The Material Dimension of Clouds

The Material Dimension of Clouds

Editing:
Lucía Egaña Rojas y Ce Quimera.

Edition:
Pluri Ediciones

With contribution by:
Tau Luna Acosta, Tatiana Avendaño, María Bajo, Romina Casile,
Anaís Córdova-Páez, Ana CSC, Lucía Egaña Rojas, val flores,
Kina Madno, Elízabeth Manjarrés Ramos, Lucrecia Masson Córdoba,
Thais de Menezes, Valeska Morales Urbina, Caro Novella,
iki yos piña funes, Ce Quimera, Natalia Rivera, Iria Rodríguez,
danele sarriugarte mochales, Pablo Selín, Roberta Stubs, Nur Tissera
y Sophia Wong.

Editorial design, cover and inside images:
Camila Gonzalez S. — @ilacami_

English translation:
Stephanie Graham

ISBN:
978-84-128020-1-6

This project has received support from the Allianz Foundation,
Mamen García Audi (State of the Arts Consulting) and the Daniel
and Nina Carasso Foundation.

First edition Barcelona, February 2024

The Material Dimension of Clouds

Pluriversidad Nómada

PLURI EDICIONES

CONTENT

MATTER, CLOUDS AND TERRITORIES

Ce Quimera and Lucía Egaña Rojas

This book is a polyhedral artefact with many sides and layers. We have written it collectively, with the intention of broadening and multiplying the ways of thinking about and dealing with the ecocide we currently inhabit. Our first objective has been tackling the material dimension of what seems to have none, knowing that in doing so we may touch upon historical memory, speculations of all sorts and abandoning human-centred matrices of analysis, amongst other outcomes.

We find ourselves in a difficult context, where the extractivism of bodies and territories has generated a situation fragmented by inequality, where countries in the global North live at the expense of the majority of those in the South, where humans, in an escalation of privileges and abuses of power that have no limits/end, ravage all the misnamed terrestrial "resources", whether human or non-human. For these issues and other equally complex problems there can be no easy answer. Nor does this book seek to provide answers and solutions, either for the present or for the future, but rather offers a plurality of voices to contribute to debates and discussions in a way that is commensurate with the complexity of the conflicts that surround us.

Pluriversidad Nómada is a project that was born of the desire to create a loving space, where practices and debates regarding the many daily issues that concern us can unfold. It seeks to be an exercise in stirring up the earth to aerate it, and see if by throwing a few seeds in, something can grow. It is a project that involves a great deal of energy, and our hands tire from working so hard, but inevitably sprouts appear in the dry soil. Moments to think together, to move our bodies, to touch this polyhedral artefact we hold in our hands. It is also a space to ask ourselves what's truly happening in a terrain that's become yet another latest trend, where art, science and technology are linked together in a superfluous, superficial way, as if robotically placing one word after another, always in the same order and giving next to no context. It is possible that we are no longer talking about these three words with our project. After almost three years since our inception, during which we've undergone mutations, and forged new alliances, possibly these words only serve an initial excuse to weave together other modes of radical pedagogies that enable pluriversal thought and action, disobeying the mandates of the academy, and undermining the supposed universality of modern Western knowledge.

With this book Pluriversidad Nómada inaugurates its own publishing house. We believe it is important to open spaces for critical thinking and expression that has historically been marginalised. We believe that the communities we inhabit produce extremely valuable and important knowledge for embracing our ways of being, and occupying the now. That is why we are very happy to begin with this book to kick off Pluri Ediciones. We hope that in the not too distant future we will be able to continue making public a number of ideas and forms of creative expression to contribute to the epistemic, social and cultural transformation that our reality demands of us.

We inaugurate the publishing house with the project "The Material Dimension of Clouds" where, as we said, we have sought to create a space to reflect on the material dimension of that which appears to be incorporeal. A space to think about how it affects bodies, territories, how it is anchored in historical memory, how we can imagine different possible futures, and what would be necessary to achieve them. With this book we are interested in opening up complex, entangled debates, where numerous and diverse themes are able to coexist for communal reflection. Working with the volatile and aerial idea of clouds also forces us to connect with the ground, as well as with what resides on the surface of the ocean and the depths below, with what can be found washed up on the shore. We are faced with a colonial and extractivist history that is not exclusively about so-called "raw materials", but about deep layers of meaning, bodies, energies, spiritualities and knowledge that continue to sustain us.

This book contains ten unpublished texts by various authors, plus four short introductions to some of the writings, through which we seek to approach the subject from complex and diverse perspectives. The currently much-used concept of "climate change" seems to us to obscure the historical implications behind it. We prefer to talk about colonialism, exploitation, extractivism. We prefer to connect with the memory of the Earth, and what inhabits it, to address this moment. In this sense, the texts are woven from fragments that form together a partial and incomplete fabric.

The text by iki yos piña narváez, "Contra-Colonial Matter", is an "exercise in critical fabulation, as an imaginative practice of symbolic self-repair in the face of the ecological disaster generated by anthropic colonialism". It is a text written from the Caribbean diaspora, as a reflexive and activating exercise in the micro-politics of resistance around black-Caribbean memory, and the damage to the non-human world inflicted by the West. It is also a text that deals with healing, alliances of living bodies and memory, the sea, gray whales and living matter.

Lucrecia Masson in "Lying Around with Cows" outlines a creative investigation of the body and animality.

She proposes, using conceptual tools, such as *Inventing Imagination,* to look around and not forward, tossing aside the basis of colonial western thought: progress. Lucrecia transports us to time *with* cows, to the slowness of rumination and to the possibility, afforded by this same slowness, of absorbing all the nutrients of food and research. "If I lie around with cows, it is to think-with them, to know-with them, and how do I account for this? Imagination is the key".

In her text "The Internet of Plants" Kina Madno asks us to reconsider the binomials of modern Western thought, in which bodies, animality and plants from the Trans*Plant project developed by Quimera Rosa also figure. Like other texts in this book, questions are raised about *becoming with* plants, and, taking another step further, considering inter-species transitions and possible incorporations with plants. In a speculative exercise about a near future where the internet no longer works, Kina invites us to connect to/explore an internet of plants that she calls "Mycorrhiza Intranet". We find ourselves moving through data networks woven with threads of plants, fungi, bacteria, minerals and topsoil in a terrain where links are made through reciprocity.

The internet is "built from the unbridled, colonial, capitalist and ecocidal exploitation of minerals" rebukes Natalia Rivera in "Internet for Bacteria", as she sums up the current world wide web, which alongside Kina Madno's text proposes multi-species alternatives to the internet as we know it today. Both texts revolve around the internet of things, a scarcity of energy, and the enormous consumption of matter and bodies (not only human ones) that using these technologies implies. What would happen if the internet ceased to exist? What would happen if we entered into a collaborative relationship with plants, fungi and bacteria to be able to communicate with them and with each other? How do we create interspecies bonds in a way that is non-colonial and non-extractivist? Natalia proposes a new/different model of relationship to create such a medium, moving away from the anthropocentric positions that currently inform technological development, in which the internet of bacteria shifts from being a technology that seeks to use these organisms as mere material support, to one that enables the emergence of Hyperconnected Bacteria, as a hybrid organism with which we co-create.

In the text by Pablo Selín and Lucía Egaña we fully engage with the materiality of clouds, their weight, their smell, their temperature, and their physical infrastructure made of metal, concrete, water and cables, where different computer systems interact, "different languages talking to each other, accepting and rejecting each other according to their own definition. Unlike the clouds in the sky, computer clouds belong to specific people, to companies, to governments". The text transports us to a pluriversal cloud where we explain the motivations behind the Pluriversidad Nómada[1] website, with which we seek to generate a pedagogical and self-explanatory site regarding the processes that occur in its operation, what happens with data flows (energetic and symbolic), so that you can truly "see" what you are looking at.

The first part of the book closes with the text by val flores "Lenguaraces of the future, breeding ruins for our visionary chaos", where pedagogical practice is presented as imaginative action. Pedagogy is ready to disorganise its own (non) knowledge: "The collective as a system for projecting ideas, the body as a working method, the word as artistic and political material, thought as aesthetics. To make other ways of life possible, languages and imagination are the experimental and inventive conditions of a pedagogical frequency".

The second part of the book is an experiment in pedagogy and speculation on the transmission of knowledge. Throughout 2023 we organised four workshops addressing the different materialities that sustain us. These workshops explored the production of new narratives around sciences, technologies, extractivism, the environmental crisis, our relationship with (so-called) "natural resources" and relationships between bodies (human and non-human), the living, and the so-called non-living.

For each of the workshops, we asked a participant to write a text that might relate or tell what happened

---

1. http://pluriversidadnomada.net

during the session, while also intersecting it with their own reflections or work. The text would not be a literal chronicle of what happened, but would rather employ the pedagogical space as a textual springboard. Through this exercise, we sought to ideate new ways of transmitting knowledge, as well as alternatives to documenting educational processes, so that they would become something other than yet another audiovisual record posted online. Our resistance to retransmit pedagogical spaces via the internet is not only due to the large amount of "invisible" resources necessary to access and produce streaming content. It also speaks to a critique of the supposed universal accessibility of everything online. Experiences during the pandemic have highlighted unequal access to the internet and devices, as well as the need for adequate spaces to be able to optimally participate in these activities. For many institutions, it is easier to stream programming online, contributing to the zoomification of life, instead of attending to the importance of relationships, or responding to the diverse needs of participants that would make a pedagogical process truly effective.

Seeking other ways of documenting a workshop is what we sought to explore through the texts commissioned from Caro Novella, danele sarriugarte and Thais de Menezes[2]. The response was powerful writing, with

2. In the case of the writing workshop, we chose to include fragments of texts produced by the participants themselves during the workshop.

unique subjective and critical perspectives that, as such, hardly managed to transmit "everything" that happened in the workshop. This was part of what we were looking for, even though we knew that the subjective writing triggered by a specific space can take us to places that even become personal. We have decided to complement the writing that emerged from the workshops with short reviews written by those who taught or directed them.

On the other hand, and in an attempt to broaden access to educational content from different territories, we have held workshops in cities throughout the kingdom of spain (Palma de Mallorca, Donostia, Barcelona and Madrid) and in collaboration with various spaces, from autonomous collectives to public and private institutions, which form part of the Pluriversidad Nómada network[3] .

Although we initially programmed four workshops, we ultimately held five, taking advantage of the Mayan collective Mujeres Ajchowen's visit to the kingdom of spain, who led the workshop "Silomen Cholq'ij". Despite falling outside of the original programme, we decided this workshop was in keeping with the pedagogical programme for "The Material Dimension of Clouds", and furthermore responded to a contingent and unplanned event a year ago. Allowing space for this workshop within the original programme meant being able to make it more porous, opening it up to what the Pluriversidad Nómada

3. https://pluriversidadnomada.net/red_y_consejo/

network might bring. At the same time, the inclusion of this fifth workshop, also meant adding a corporeal dimension to the work done by our Institutes[4] whose objectives relate to the Mujeres Ajchowen. The workshop held by this collective provided a space where the artistic practice and manifestations of the Mayan people merged with everyday life. Through the framework of five concrete energies of the calendar, our comrades led work bound to healing, Mother Earth, water and other natural elements that are necessary to sustain life.

The four workshops originally programmed were "Atlas Cuir - SF Trans*Plant", given by Ce Quimera, where self-experimentation, the cultivation of symbiotic beings, changes in the scale of vision, microscopic worlds and the frontiers between the living and the non-living were explored. Tatiana Avendaño and Anaís Córdova-Páez explored the possibility of expanding the capacity to emit and receive signals from bodies through with the workshop "Ca2= radiating what speech doesn't capture", weaving relationships between different species, knowledge and times. Tau Luna Acosta, who led "Listening to a Rock", proposed a series of exercises in speculative archaeology to trace extractive drifts and migratory maps through the shared listening and reading of scientific texts, fiction and Indigenous wisdom, as a way of tracing the migratory history of minerals present in our everyday

4. https://pluriversidadnomada.net/institutos/

lives. Lucía Egaña in the workshop "Confabulating and Imagining the End of This World" proposed a space for speculative writing about the future, present and past to come, to create new (im) possible places for the healing of broken imaginaries.

Throughout the book we have respected the pronouns and citations that the respective author of each text decided to use. We have also respected the forms of naming territories and gentilicism when applicable. We consider that each person has their own particular ways of describing the world, and we believe it is important to respect this right to pluriversality.

This introduction was written between October and November 2023, with our four hands divided between the territories called Mexico, Germany, the kingdom of spain and France, now having watched, for over a month, the genocide of the Palestinian people by the Israeli government and militia live on the internet, with the US government and the majority of European governments complicit. What is happening in Palestine is an ethnic cleansing that started not just over a month ago, but rather 75 years ago. The internet has not yet reached the entire planet, but through it we have access to the massacre of an entire people live. Writing about this does not bring about a ceasefire, nor does it stop the bombing of a whole culture into oblivion, but we want to remember and record what is happening, as part of the archive that this book is beginning to become. If we do not talk about this, we risk writing an introductory text burdened with a sense of impotence or banality. As migrants from Abya Yala who live in Fortress Europe, we say:

Not in our name.

Don't stop talking about Palestine.

We want territories, not borders.

PART I

00 km

COUNTER-COLONIAL MATTER

iki yos piña narváez

> *I was because I was before.*
> *so that I will be and will be again*
> Kimbwandènde Kia

I write this text immersed in a movement of retro-action, immersed in the infinite vectors of the flight of a "chronosophy in spirals"[5], from a maroon body escaping the cisgenerity that forms part of the prison system as colonial technology. A body embraced and blessed by the guaichía and olokum.

This little text has the vitality of an ancestral body, and at the same time a body altered by biohacking through plants that alter my hormonal system, and one altered by necro-pharma-politics. This text is written from S-pain,

5. See Martins, Leda Maria. Performance do tempo espiralar: Poeticas do corpo-tela (2021) Edit Cobogó.

where I have to renew a "humanitarian permit" every 8 months to "live" on this plantation that has a whole anti-blackness technology to deter black bodies from arriving in this territory.

I write this text from the Caribbean diaspora, and it is an exercise in reflection, one in movement, thinking and feeling the memories of the black and brown Caribbean, the residues and existing connections between the insep-arability of matter and the ancestral living unknown to the rationalising disciplines of the West. This reflective exercise is an outline of several unfinished ideas sur-rounding black and brown Caribbean memory, the sea, transatlantic abduction, the damage to the world of the non-human inflicted by the West, healing, and alliances of living bodies and living matter as micro-political actions of counter-colonial resistance.

we are matter

Quibayo is a natural, spiritual temple where the forces of physics and metaphysics converge. It is a space of ancestral preservation of black and maroon lives, fugitives from the plantation of lives-matter. In Quimbayo, bodies are mat-ter, they are mediums for articulation of the orishas, Loas, the orí and the infinite constellation of egbé orum, which converge there. To understand the body as matter is to try to understand a geophysical dimension of the com-position of black-brown bodies and the inseparability of resident time, as C. Sharpe would say. The potentially-subhuman subhuman bodies that inhabit the historical-structural underline of the zone of "being", in Fanonian terms. To understand the body as matter is to try to understand a geophysical dimension of the body in time.

In the wake[6] are matter-bodies. A matter-body is a body that travels in non-linear time. A matter-body does not return to the plantation. It transcends the trauma, but remembers the trauma. A matter-body lives in the present of a social death, but manages to "transport" itself. It manages to become the smoke of tobacco, the smell of rue and the sound of sixteen cowries my mother dropped on the ground for an overview of the non-obvious world.

A matter-body, a maroon body is a body that has been configured with biological particles that have travelled through time. The fugitive bodies that escaped in the transatlantic mass capture by white supremacy, live on in sediments of sand, in corals and in the memory of the sand, in an underwater and terrestrial ecosystem, as ancestral matter that has been part of the dance of the Gray Whales, where the iodine of sea salt fused with the iodine of the blood of fugitive black bodies.

Alexis P. Gumbs talks about "intimacy with Atlantic gray whales who became extinct shortly after the era of the transatlantic theft complex, and how the bones of those who did not survive, those who were thrown or

---

6. See Christina Sharpe, In the Wake: On Blackness and Being (2016) Duke University Press.

those who jumped, became part of the sediment gray whales filter on the seafloor of an underwater ecosystem", of course. This is when C. Sharpe speaks of resident time. And C. Sharpe thinks of resident time in relation to the intimacy of the Atlantic gray whales, and how those falling black bodies and whales were becoming part of that underwater ecosystem that is still alive with us[7]. For me they are matter-bodies - trans-species of escape, of anti-colonial action.

> *"Gray Whales are world shapers. The only large whale to feed on sediment on the bottom of the ocean, they leave massive troughs on the underwater surface of the Earth. They dig up nutrients that feed whole ecosystems. And they have been missing from the Atlantic Ocean since the end of the transatlantic slave trade. What happened? Marine biologists say it is still a mystery why the Atlantic population of Gray Whales went extinct. Is it possible that whalers on enslaving ships killed Gray Whales and didn't report it? Was there already a smaller population of Gray Whales than they had thought? Miscalculation and under-documentation are the theories so far. And no one mentions the timing of the transatlantic slave trade as relevant to the extinction of Atlantic Gray Whales. But me. I won-*

7. See: Christina Sharpe, Alexis Pauline Gumbs. On Water, Salt, Whales, and the Black Atlantics, 2021. https://thefunambulist.net/magazine/the-ocean/on-water-salt-whales-and-the-black-atlantics

der. Yes. I wonder if the toxicity of the slave trade and its impact on the ocean have been under-reported. Lucille Clifton says "the Atlantic is a sea of bones." What is the half-life of the transubstantiation of life into servitude? Does it ever dissolve? And the bones of those captives who freed themselves, or left their bodies and were subsequently thrown overboard became what? Filtered ultimately into the baleen of the Atlantic Gray whale, right? So there is actually a digestive truth to the idea that the ancestors we lost in the transatlantic slave trade became whales. Is sediment sentient? Kriti Sharma is embarking on an underwater research project about deep sea sediment that might be countering methane to rebalance the planet. Don't sleep on sediment, at the bottom, knowledge grows. And maybe there is more to the interspecies relation. Could there have been an interspecies pact between those who would not survive the transatlantic slave trade. Could it be that a refusal to survive the slave trade could be transferred between species? Did the Gray Whales act out of solidarity refusing the terms of a betrayal they held in their stomachs. Or, since researchers have recently discovered that Gray Whales can migrate between the Atlantic and Pacific Oceans, did the Atlantic Gray Whales simply leave the Atlantic in response to their intimate knowledge...".[8]

8. Text by Alexis P. Gumbs on her Instagram account: https://www.instagram.com/p/B1wBjwBg1qD/?hl=es

Anti-colonial living matter alliance

The intimacy of matter reaches domestic places and the rituality of diasporic bodies. Think of the passage of a cowrie - búzios, petaw, ebambara - in the Atlantic Ocean, think of the iodine in the salt, the iodine in the blood and the bone residues in these snails present on the ifá board, and at the fire festival in Quibayo.

My mother is also matter, that is also what they call bodies of those who are mediums. A matter-body is a body in connection with what the world cannot see. A matter-body is a body in connection "with what the sand remembers"[9], with what the sea "remembers", with what the rocks remember. In Quibayo my mother walked barefoot on red coals, matter on matter. Coal is also matter, like that of black bodies, and Indigenous people moved from one continent to another as "raw material".

I am matter. Before I started my diaspora again, my mother gave me the búzios she used to wear. I always kept them with me until I lost them in one of my many moves to Europe. I have always insisted on drawing them as a way of recovering what was torn away. The snails are in my body and in my memory. The búzios inhabit me and I inhabit this world as a way of being in the *in between* of this world to which I do not belong, but at the same time I belong.

9. Vanessa Agard-Jones. What the Sands Remember. GLQ (2012) 18 (2-3): 325-346, Duke University Press.

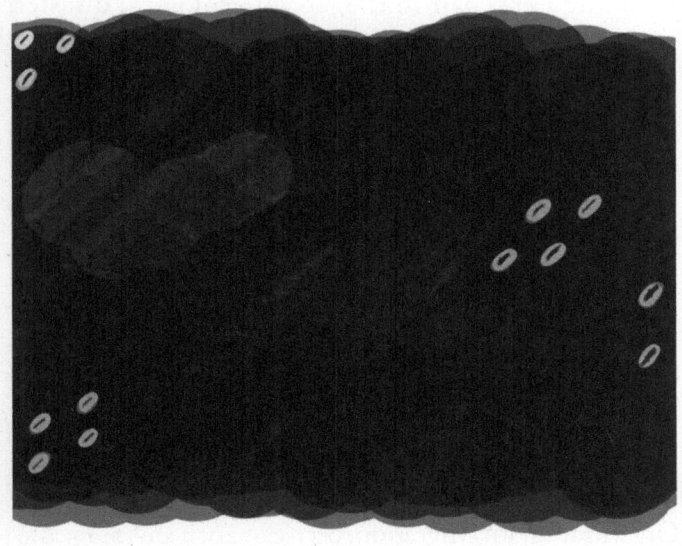

MATTER. BY IKI YOS PIÑA

imagine if the transatlantic slave trade had not happened. imagine if the idea of development from colonial theft, the accumulation of capital had not happened. imagine if geological time marked our lives and not the arrow of time. imagine if the notion of nature-culture as a colonial binomial had not marked our existence. imagine if the idea of nature had not required the idea of ecology as a reparative fiction for living matter-earth.

This is not an exercise in romanticisation. It is an exercise in critical fabulation, as an imaginative practice of symbolic self-repair in the face of ecological disaster, generated by anthropic colonialism.

Gladis is one of a group of Orca whales that in 2023 attacked more than 50 sailing ships off the coast of Gibraltar. In 2022, it is estimated that 2,390 people drowned in the Mediterranean off the Spanish coast. It is only an estimation, because their bodies are not being sought. 2,390 murders at the hands of Europe's elected governments that go unpunished. 2,390 lives to which are added the more than 500,000 people who are now waiting for #RegularisationNow of their papers in Spain[10].

29 August 2022. Nearly 19,000 people in migration processes are considered to have gone missing on the Mediterranean sea route, according to the International Organization for Migration, between 2014 and 2019, and 3,300 in 2021 en route to Europe. Only 13% of the bodies have been recovered and therefore identified as deceased[11].

10. Such as, for example, the "Top Manta" collective. Collective of migrants of African origin, mainly along the southern borders of Spain. The website of the collective is: https://topmanta.store

11. https://www2.cruzroja.es/-/cruz-roja-implanta-un-proyecto-de-identificaci-c3-b3n-de-personas-desaparecidas-en-ruta-migratoria-por-v-c3-ada-mar-c3-adtima

We are the earthquake // Black elDorado

In 2020 I started an artistic and research residency in Paris with Jota Mombaça, thinking about the anti-colonial geological dimension of European extractivism. Stones have life: Pyrite, the so-called fool's gold, served as protection to prevent the theft of several gold reserves. Rocks heal and have memory.

For the Museo Madre in Naples exhibition Rethinking Nature[12], we created an installation presenting two audio-visual works showing this simultaneous relationship between extractivism and healing in terms of contact with geological and biological materiality.

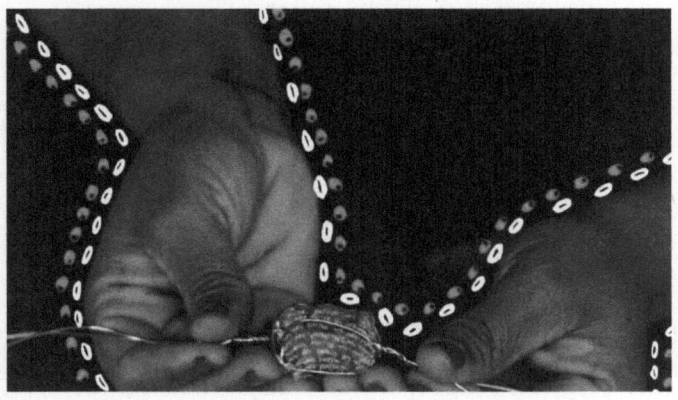

FRAME VIDEO INSTALLATION. 2021. WE ARE THE EARTHQUAKE

12. For more information on the project, please consult the following link: https://www.madrenapoli.it/en/jota-mombaca-iki-yos-pina-narvaez/

Black El Dorado (We are the earthquake) is a poethical and political speculative exercise on the intricate relation of black-Indigenous bodies, the constitution of the geological regime of modernity and the radical fugitivity of Pyrite (Fool's Gold). We believe that, by experiencing our bodies as ancestral matter, we are able to articulate the dense and violent histories of extraction that are inscribed in colonised land, as well as to connect with the infinite potential for healing and earthly resilience that form our anti-colonial lives and desires. In this sense, we are interested in ways of reading colonial narratives through its breaches, looking for deviant forms of agency that challenge modern-colonial conceptions of time, nature and power.

Healing matter

The poetics of matter generates a process of connection with bodies. Time-travelling bodies. Bodies marked at birth. When you are a body-matter you manage not to divide the outside from the inside, you manage to establish a physical and metaphysical inseparability. Quibayo, that place of ancestral refuge where matter-bodies are transported and receive spiritual entities, strengthen their orí and manage to dance, dialogue and kiss fire, coal, pyrite, jet, búzios, coral and the sediments of the sea. This matter resists anthropic actions in geological time, this matter has a memory that is against colonialism.

LYING AROUND WITH COWS
[A Research Scene as an Exercise in Imagination]

Lucrecia Masson Córdoba

The route I propose with this text is to open up an exercise in imagination departing from a research scene. I want to talk about a practice that is my body researching with cows. What I offer here is possibly an opening of what happened, while assuming the partiality of said opening, that is to say, making room as well for what possibly happened that I couldn't see. I have brought some conceptual tools, which I think of as openers. Like a corkscrew, like a can opener. Something whose utility is so completely part of "x" situation that it becomes essential, something that can't be thought of without those things it can open. I imagine the opener together with the objects it opens, while at the same time -surely some- of its possible uses escape me, as it isn't possible to know entirely: I won't know until the moment it's time to take the opener out.

This text addresses how I applied this strategy in research with -what I thought were just cows- but they were cows, and not only cows. This scene is part of my broader research in which I propose a creative investigation of the body and animality. I've been working with ruminants[13] for years, specifically with cows. Through a transdisciplinary approach I explore the possibility of a ruminant onto-epistemology, starting from the cow and its excess (of meat and not only)[14] together with the territory. Rumination, as a regurgitating movement involving the passage from one stomach to another, invites a process where the beginning and the end of nutritive action are blurred. It's a complex digestive system that, favoured by slowness, enables skilful use of the food, even if the pasture is not very nutritious or the grass is in short supply. I am therefore interested in the gesture of lying down, and in the fact that it is slowness that makes it possible to absorb nutrients. This is the gesture we are pursuing.

13. The ruminant animals possibly most familiar to humans are bovids (cattle, sheep, goats and antelopes), deer, giraffes and their relatives.

14. About the "not only" concept see De la Cadena, M. 2014. Runa: Human but *not only. HAU: Journal of ethnographic Theory 4(2)* and subsequent works by the author.

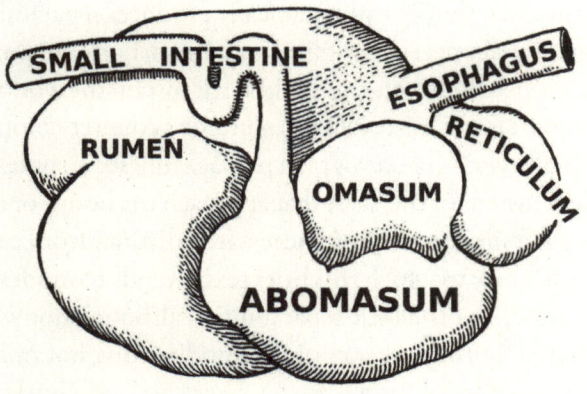

ANATOMY OF THE RUMINANT STOMACH.

#1. InventionResearch

> *Far from being a rigid task with a*
> *pre-established format, research is actually*
> *a form of imagination and care.*
> *Escrituras geológicas (A geological writing)*, Cristina Rivera Garza

Theory is also a place of imagination. Denise Ferreira da Silva, Afro-Brazilian philosopher and artist, often positions her theorisations as artistic creations; she creates artefacts that - like pieces of art - are used in theoretical productions. Disobeying the mandate of separability -

which she names as one of the pillars of modern thought[15] - Ferreira da Silva generates theory that is also art.

If modern thought systematically produces separability - separability between disciplines or human/non-human, in this case - to disobey the binomials that sustain the world as we know it is an anti-colonial gesture, or a counter-colonial one, in the words of iki yos piña narváez funes[16]. To unlearn the pretensions of the West that approach the body - or animals - as a single entity and necessarily distinct from each other, is a task to which this brief text intends to modestly contribute. To dismantle separabilities, although not with the aim of uniting or generating hybridisations, but rather, following Marisol de la Cadena, I seek to "'un"-separate, which is not the same as uniting"[17]. It is not a question of seeking equality in what we want to approach, what interests me is a commitment to the incommensurable: how to work with things that are not measurable in relation to each other? I have tried to do some of this in my work with cows. The challenge is in continuity, the continuum

15. Ferreira da Silva works with the idea of three pillars of modern thought, namely separability, determinacy and sequentiality. See "On Difference without Separability", Catalogue from the 32nd São Paulo Art Biennial Incerteza Viva, 2016, p. 57-65.

16. iki yos piña narváez funes contributed this concept in her piece for this book.

17. The opening of the *Seres-Rios* festival (2-10 August 2021, Minas Gerais, Brazil) was a wonderful conversation between Ailton Krenak and Marisol de la Cadena, in which she discussed this idea.

of everything that exists (and by existing we are not only talking about the living). Elvira Espejo Ayca[18] is a visual artist, weaver and narrator of the oral tradition of her place of origin, an ayllu in Oruro, Bolivia, who proposes mutual nurturing:

> *In our communities there is no hierarchical rationality, but words and concepts that we use: reading with your fingers, reading with your body or reasoning with the sensitivity of your body, of your feet. It is the interconnectivity of feeling and thinking. They cannot be separated. Sensing and thinking are united, as the sentipensante.*
>
> *In Aymara: Amta yarachh uywaña, which is the mutual nurturing of thoughts and feelings.*
>
> *I cultivate thoughts, and thoughts reside within my body, within the landscape, within the instruments that are going to intervene. [...] You yourself are not the rationaliser, but rather you have required connectivities, experiences and sensibilities to be able to generate this amta yaracch aywaña, this shared thought, which leads you to new creativities[19].*

In another of her works, Denise Ferreira da Silva talks about experiments in thought that show what is possible

---

18. Elvira Espejo Ayca also speaks Quechua and Aymara and runs the Museum of Ethnography and Folklore in La Paz, Bolivia.

19. Espejo Ayca, E. 2023. *Yanak Uywaña* - La crianza mutua de las artes. Santa Fé: Imperfect fordistas. P. 8-9.

to contemplate when instead of Understanding we allow ourselves to be guided by Imagination[20]. In this way the author shifts the axis and calls for Imagination and not Understanding, both written in capital letters, to guide the experiment. If I lie around with cows, it is to think-with them, to know-with them, and how can I account for that? Imagination[21], then, is the way.

#2. Breadth invocation

Some time ago, while doing my Mondongo Exercise I said:

My approach to working/doing with cows has to do with the fact that I grew up among them. It was the excess (of meat and not only) and the slowness that initially drove me. This impulse remains a desire and a commitment that moves in two directions that, I bet, are in dialogue with each other. On the one hand, it is about approaching cosmopolitical conversations where distinctions between human and natural realms do not pre-exist: I seek to perceive those boundaries/tensions between the two worlds (human and animal). On the other hand, I renew the insistence that one cannot think without the body, and that the body exceeds what Western modernity defines as

20. In Ferreira da Silva, D. 2019. *A dívida impagável*. São Paulo: Oficina de Imaginação Política e Living Commons. P. 151.

21. From now on, in the spirit proposed by Ferreira da Silva, Imagination will appear in capital letters.

such. In that place, in the middle of these two ideas, lies the obstination that mobilises my work.[22]

It is by insisting on the resounding place of the body that we find this scene. So, opener in hand, we are entering into a scene of investigation and a device of observation. This work is one of slow observation that I carried out over a period of two months in Ombucta (Argentina), a region bordering on Patagonia, known as the dry pampa. It is an area characterised by sparse vegetation of brownish greens, by strong winds that stir the earth. It is also the place where I grew up and where my family lives and works. The days - those two months - could have been the same as any others, but now there was a willingness to observe, an intention; what had changed was attention, or the intensity of attention. I dedicated myself to sharing day after day - for approximately six hours a day, distributed in different time slots - time and space with six cows and everything that surrounds them/everything that creates them: six mother cows, their children, a bull, many other animals, the wind, the drought, among so many other entities/characters. During this exercise I sought to look around and not forward. The research scene that I am presenting/unfolding here is part of those days. In this scene there are animals, there are human animals and

22. Masson Córdoba, L. 2022. "Mondongo exercise". In *Escrituras rumiantes. Cuerpo, exceso, animalidad*. Bogotá: Pajarera libertaria. P. 37.

there are also certain dispositions that made it possible to get closer. Juliana Fausto says, in her *La cosmopolítica de los animales (Cosmopolitics of Animals)*, that she is convinced that only through multi-species encounters situated with others is it possible to devise cosmic and not exterminatory policies[23].

The place I was observing - or ethnographing - is perfectly familiar to me, the work I was doing is also familiar to me, I always have done it, and I have always shared it with cows. But, in keeping with Anna Tsing[24], the arts of observation now came into play.

ECHADAS. OMBUCTA, FEBRUARY 2021. COURTESY OF THE AUTHOR.

23. Fausto, J. 2023. *La cosmopolítica de los animales*. Buenos Aires: Cactus. P. 16.

24. Tsing, A. 2021. *La seta del fin del mundo*. Madrid: Capitán Swing.

In addition to slow observation, I sought a slow and cow-like passage of time; my initial aim was an investigation into cow time, I wanted to explore the possibility of inhabiting cow time. But the issue that became central had to do with throwing myself out, with abandoning the bipedal form. If I laid down (as cows do) everything changed a lot. The bipedal position was not at all beneficial, and as I realised that lying down was the best thing to do, and over the course of the days, we achieved a different relationship, I would say a more comfortable, more habitable one. At the beginning they were enormously interested in me, basically our relationship consisted of us looking at each other: I looked at them and they looked at me, this went on for hours. Tirelessly, insistently. However, as the days went by, I stopped being interesting to them. They no longer looked at me, but I looked at them. I looked at them and not only at them.

Two months went by lying around with the cows. Then, as the hours passed and the days went by, other characters began to "appear". And they didn't really appear, because it wasn't that they didn't exist, but rather that I couldn't see them. I had grown up on those same lands and I returned to them with a certain frequency throughout my adult life, but there was still a lot to see. A payada[25] - a popular rural

25. Song that is normally improvised, and typical of rural areas. In Chile it is known as a paya.

song - says "I walked many leagues to see what I used to look at but didn't see"[26].

Abandoning the bipedal form not only made it possible for other animals to appear, but also for ant trails to appear, other plants to appear; slow observation made it possible. Suddenly a whole series of worlds proliferated. And even the hairy armadillo[27] appeared before my eyes.

Yes, following Vinciane Despret, it is a question of inventing devices of research[28], and in my case, the device was my body. Despret speaks of setting about the task of creating devices for each investigation, and not starting from pre-existing places, not assuming with which tools I am going to investigate this or that. My shared time with cows demanded that I look. To look slowly and broadly at what this terrain is like, and from there invent ways of approaching it. We are standing before an invocation of breadth that looks around, and not forward, and that from that place seeks to perform the gesture of deacti-

26. Legua is a unit of measurement that delimits approximately five kilometres. Naming distances in terms of leagues is the most common way of speaking in the more rural areas of the region.

27. The hairy or big armadillo is one of the largest and most common of its kind in South America.

28. Vinciane Despret interviewed by Pablo Méndez for the exhibition Simbiología. Video available at youtube.com/watch?v=BqIwJJ12sGcs. *Simbiología. Prácticas artísticas en un planeta en emergencia*, ran from 6 October 2021 to 26 June 2022 at the Centro Cultural Kirchner, Buenos Aires, Argentina.

vating, at least a little, the idea of progress. In the words of Anna Tsing:

> *Progress is also implicit in a number of generally accepted assumptions about what it means to be human. Although we disguise it with other terms, such as* action, consciousness and intention, *we are told again and again that humans are different from the rest of the living world because we look forward, meaning that other species, living in the day to day, are dependent on us. As long as we continue to imagine that humans are* made *by progress, non-humans will also be trapped in that imaginative framework. [...]*
>
> *Progress is a forward march that pulls other kinds of time into its own rhythms. Without that driving beat we could perceive other temporal patterns.*
>
> *[...] disregarding where we are going allows us to look for everything we've ignored because it could never fit into the timeline of progress.*[29]

The observation that I am interested in activating in this scene does not look like progress, nor does it pretend to discover. There is no intention to produce novelty. The little ant trails, the parrots, the hairy armadillos, is it that now there are more of them, is it that they have proliferated? Weren't they already in view and I've just noticed?

29. Tsing, A. Ibid. p. 42-43.

It's simply that I could finally see them. They were always there and I didn't see. Reading a short text written by the astronomer Armando Mudrik, the idea of discovery assumes the existence of a unique reality[30].

So I invoke breadth, I look in a circular way - unlearning looking forward, unlearning progress - and I lie around with cows. The little ant trails are not my discoveries, they are not new. We've been able to see each other, we've been able to relate.

#3. Everything that was there already

I learn many things from the ruminant gesture. Things like rumination's condition of regurgitating to pass through the stomachs once again, taking its time, that if it doesn't happen calmly it can't happen. All of this then, everything that has been said so far, is about moving through the places again. Not to discover, but to walk-with, to see what was there and was not seen, to establish a relationship.

In general, we investigate what we don't know, or we follow a path that has as its starting point a departure from one place in order to arrive at another point. In this case it's rather a question of going back again, of chewing once more. It's a question - following the anti-colonial commitment I spoke of at the beginning - of trying to

30. Mudrik, A. 2023. Muchos cielos. *Hojas especulativas*, 4, Laboratorio de Antropología Especulativa.

deactivate the temporality of progress. I say deactivate while trying to avoid the trap of grandiloquence, because I don't know what it would be like to turn off the progress button, but I do know of things that can be attempted. That ResearchInvention can be done; blessed is the root[31] that "un"-separates these words. That we can rehearse a cosmopolitics that connects wind, drought, cows, sky, furry people and the smell of poop covered with little flies. That it is a matter of letting Imagination be the guide.

31. Translator's note: In the original in Spanish, Research (Investigación) and Invention (Invento) share the same root.

THE INTERNET OF PLANTS

Kina Madno

By way of introduction, let us begin with some figures related to the representativeness of humans, things and plants on what we call the internet. When searching the "internet of things"[32] in Google, we receive: "Approximately 1,520,000,000 results (0.38 seconds). For the "internet of plants": "Approximately 386,000,000,000 results (0.27 seconds)".

With regard to these figures, we must keep in mind that plants represent 98% of the Earth's biomass, thereby nullifying calling it "our" planet. And as for the current

---

32. "The internet of things (IoT) is the process of connecting every-day physical items to the internet: from common household objects, such as light bulbs, to health care resources, such as medical devices; to smart personal wearables and accessories; and even smart city systems". http://redhat.com/es/topics/internet-of-things/what-is-iot

operating model, that of the Internet is extractivist and competitive (or rather productivist / extractivist-colonial)[33]. And therefore, completely unequal in terms of production, function and access.

The internet of plants, on the other hand, is based on mutualistic symbiosis[34] between its different agents, thereby making life possible.

Literally, in order to situate this body of knowledge, my research/elaboration of the internet of plants was

33. "I do not intend to carry out an exhaustive and full overlook, but rather to analyse the convergences that give rise to the increasingly visible struggles and resistance of women against patriarchy, extractivism and colonialism / neoliberalism in Latin America. The aim is to reflect on how gender has been articulated through - and produced the visibility of - the anti-extractivist struggle, not only because it was and is massively mobilised by women, but also because the very demands and understandings of gender (from different theoretical, political and institutional influences) particularise and strengthen these movements, especially when they intersect with the dimensions of ethnicity, race and class. To this end, I seek to analyse three dimensions that converge in what today can be seen as an anti-extractivist women's movement in Latin America", Melisa (2022). Movimiento de mujeres contra el extractivismo: feminismos y saberes multisituados en convergencia. Debate Feminista, 32, 64: e2287. https://doi.org/10.22201/cieg.2594066xe.2022.64.2287

34. According to Wikipedia"Mutualism is a biological interaction between individuals of different species, where both benefit and improve their biological fitness. Similar actions that occur between members of the same species are called cooperation. Mutualism differs from other interactions in which one species benefits at the expense of one or more other species; these are cases of exploitation, such as parasitism, predation, etc."

developed for the Trans*Plant project[35], with its central axis based on the creation and intravenous administration of chlorophyll. In order to exist, this project, beyond technical-scientific knowledge, needed/wanted to create a science-fiction universe in which it could fully have/make meaning(s). It is precisely this expression that is embodied in the bio-hacking magazine *Ni Urras Ni Anarres* published on 08 March 2039[36]. The journey of walking through grades of past-present-future time (whatever the order in which these "times" are delineated) responds to this need. Is it possible to imagine life without (the desire to) tell stories? Is there a difference between a "reconstructed" past and an "imagined" future to nourish/live the "present"? Is it desirable to live without asking questions? Especially if they are these basic ones. Basic. Common. Simple. Complex. Radical.

If you wish to set the mood for reading this text, either solo or with company, you can do so by taking a few shots of liquid chlorophyll. We aim to shape the reading in the form of a mycorrhiza, by means of agency on (vegetable) paper as its support, which seeks to send down roots. May the Chlorophyll be with/in you.

---

35. For more information on the project, please visit the following link: http://quimerarosa.net/transplant/

36. All parts of this indented text come from the article published in said magazine, also called "Ni Urras ni Anarres" (Neither Urras nor Anarres) by its contributors/readers.

2024. 08 March. Earth's annual resources have already been exhausted. The equivalent of four planets are needed to satisfy human consumption. Working from a private virtual network of the second internet, a group of biohackers called Q.R*3 decides to try to connect to the mycorrhiza, a network composed of the symbiosis between roots and fungi through which the terrestrial plant world communicates.

Their goal: to enter into a collaboration with plants to try to reverse the situation. The first members of this group soon died under the effect of an unknown molecule. Nothing is known about the rest of the group. Or very little...

"If we had devoted as much research to communicating with trees as we have devoted to the extraction and use of oil, perhaps we could light a city through photosynthesis, or we could feel plant sap running through our veins, but our western civilisation has specialised in capital and domination, in taxonomy and identification, not cooperation and mutation".[37]

Year 2036, 26 February. By that date the available annual resources of planet Earth had already been exhausted. The human way of life of the Global North already needed six planets to satisfy its consumption. On 8 March, numerous transnational and intersectional revolts

37. Paul B. Preciado. Un apartamento en Urano (An Apartment on Uranus). Ed. Anagrama, 2019.

erupted across the planet, combining various physical and virtual actions, many of them in conjunction with each other. One of its most remarkable effects was the collapse of the network then called the internet; the rarefaction of mineral resources had already made its maintenance more complex and its administration even more authoritarian. On 8 March, mineral extraction mines were occupied and re-appropriated by their workers and neighbouring populations, undersea cables were cut, and many data centres were attacked through the network itself and from the street. On 13 March, the internet was shut down.

The multi-agent, ecosystemic dimension of photosynthesis is based on a return on consumption, where those who consume energy return it transformed. A synergy that guarantees sustainability. A form of permanent and circular barter.

And when we say photosynthesis, we are simplifying (perhaps by only considering what is of obvious interest to humans), because there are two types:

▷ Oxygenic photosynthesis, which produces useful sugars for the plant and, in turn, consumes carbon dioxide (CO_2) and under-produces oxygen (O_2). This type is essential for respiration, as it works by reverse gas exchange.

▷ Anoxygenic photosynthesis, which does not produce oxygen (O_2), but uses sunlight to break down hydrogen sulphide molecules (H_2S). In this way, it releases sulphur into the environment or accumulates it inside the bacteria that are capable of carrying the process out.

In order to understand the Micorriza Intranet Connection *project, it seems important to us to situate both the group and the context of its actions.*

The Trans*Plant (T*P) group, like the networks of which it was a part, was made up of transfeminist, non-binary and gender-dissident interweavers in alliance with activists, artists, scientists and hackers. Their beginnings in biohacking hark back to the late 2000s, in the postporn community located at N 41° 22' 47.112", E 2° 10'14.385" in which BDSM *practices were central. Their affinity for latex gloves, needles, scalpels or ropes is key to understanding their unabashed approach to tattooing, nursing practices and biomedical experimentation in kitchens, garages and laboratories. All these practices were closely linked to self-experimentation and what was then known as* DIY / DIWO *(do it yourself / do it with others). Although T*P defined itself as a nomadic and transnational group, it was mostly made up of people from Abya Yala who had migrated to Europe and Europeans.*

Their work on extractivism, colonisation and witch-hunting led them to cross the Atlantic again in 2012 heading towards S 17° 22' 56.889", W 66° 9' 52.364" to join the Akelarre Yaku project[38] with Maria F. D., for their

---

38. http://akelarreyaku.tumblr.com

first direct connection with plants and the molecular. It is in this context that their research on the cinchona tree, the extraction of quinine, malaria, and the birth of the pharmaceutical industry began.

2015. It's the time of COP 21, and its committee of experts inaugurate a new geological era: the Anthropocene era, characterised by human activity that has altered the Earth's natural cycle. Global warming, nuclear crises, dramatic decline in biodiversity, human and non-human climate refugees... There's no doubt about it. However, Donna Haraway warns us of the primary danger of the term Anthropocene: the very notion of anthropos, based on "human exceptionalism and methodological individualism"[39], reminding us that all forms of life will seek their own solution to get out of this crisis, so no way out will be possible without collaboration between them[40].

---

39. Donna J. Haraway. Seguir con el problema: Generar parentesco en el Chthuluceno (Staying with the Trouble: Making Kin in the Chthulucene). Ed. Consonni, 2019.

40. "I am also interested in what plants can teach us about how to live well on this planet. I have coined the term 'plantropocene' as an antidote to the anthropocentric concept of the anthropocene, in the hope that we can aspire to move out of the extractive and exploitative relationships with nature that are rapidly accelerating our decline. The plantropocene aspires to create an era in which people learn once and for all to collaborate with plants. Check out my new article, which looks at photosynthesis as the missing link we must all learn as we try to fight the apocalyptic future promised by anthropocene thinking." Interview with Natasha Myers. http://naukas.com/2016/04/13/entrevista-con-natasha-myers/

After the internet crashed on 13 March 2036, the Trans*Plant group decided to launch the first attempt to connect to Mycorrhiza, a network composed of the symbiosis of roots and fungi through which the terrestrial plant world communicates[41]. It took 20 years of preparation to get there. Its aim was to establish a tool for direct communication with the plant world, with the hope of generating a post-anthropos alliance. To establish a connection point with the mycorrhiza, they had set up their servers using accumulated recycled materials creating a mini-internet of their own. The aim of the first test was to generate an initial direct connection point at a specific location on Mycorrhiza, and establish a remote connection with a T*P server, in order to obtain parts of information exchanged, and try to work out a translation code in human language. This first test was entrusted to the QR*3 group, who in 2036 set up camp at N 41° 39' 59.7", W 0° 53' 58.1", where the river's drought had

---

41. Most plant systems grow on this symbiotic association in which the fungus supplies the plant with inorganic compounds such as nitrogen or phosphorus, needed by the plant for nutrition and growth, and the plant provides the fungus with sugars resulting from photosynthesis," explains the scientist about these networks, which some researchers have called the "internet of plants" because of their similarity to network nodes (...). Although the entire scientific community acknowledges the importance of these interactions that occur in mycorrhizae, controversy arose when Simard referred to these connections as the 'wisdom of the forest'. As a result, other researchers have shed light on this web of underground pipes in the form of roots and hyphae (cylindrical filaments of the fungal body), which can be kilometres long and occur in all climate systems". http://agenciasinc.es/Reportajes/Las-comunicaciones-secretas-de-las-plantas

exposed large Mycorrhiza caves. The remote connection node was established, not far away, at level -3 at N 41° 39' 35.432", W 0° 54' 27.387". It is also known that QR*3 named this site "the Bunker", "the Incubator" or "the -3".

The connection point was successfully implemented, but the first members of this group soon died due to the effects of a volatile molecule, the identity of which remains unknown. They didn't know at the time that the process would lead them to another type of connection with the plant: the administration of intravenous chlorophyll to their participants...

It's known that this remote connection node is still alive, although its current location is unknown. It's also known that there were several versions of its configuration as it evolved, one of them being a change of plants to ensure its functioning and security. In the first version Micorriza took the form of a Milpa, a farming system used in some territories of Abya Yala.

We also know that Micorriza required multiple criteria from the QR*3 group to establish the security of the initial remote connection node. Two of these were:

▷ This node must be located in a bunker so that no one can detect it.
▷ This node must have a security system in case of intrusion into the bunker, which is to be monitored by Micorriza. This system is based on the release of volatile molecules whose composition remains secret, and

depends on the behaviour of the intruders. Thanks to elements provided by T*P (photographs, diagrams, texts and fragments of code), we've been able to reconstruct one of the last versions of this connection node. For this purpose, we've received an Artemisia Annua seed cryopreserved in 2019 at N 47° 17' 48.046", E 2° 30' 35.319".

In this reconstructed version, the Milpa has been replaced by Artemisia, a plant used for thousands of years to treat malaria, a disease now endemic across Terra (Earth) due to global warming. The T*P group's link to seed cryopreservation is explained in detail in Open the Seed. One of the conditions set by T*P when they gave us these files was not to publish any information, only some images of the reconstruction, as well as a bit of information on how it works. We've only been allowed to publish a partially decoded fragment of the text issued by Micorriza.

NI URRAS NI ANARRES - MICROSCOPIC VIEW OF MYCORRHIZAE - QUIMERA ROSA

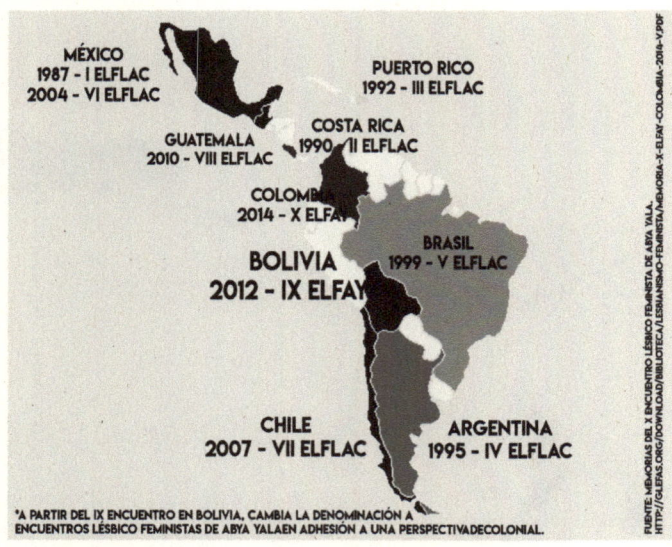

THIS MAP OF LESBIAN FEMINIST GATHERINGS IN ABYA YALA WAS DRAWN UP BY AUTONOMOUS LESBIANS FROM THE STATE OF SÃO PAULO WHO CALL THEMSELVES LESBOFEMINISTS, WHO ARE IN ONGOING CONTACT WITH, AND ARE CONTINUOUSLY REFLECTING ON, WHAT AFFECTS AND UNITES THEM WITHIN LATIN AMERICA. THEY HAVE DEDICATED THEMSELVES TO A LESBO-CENTRED AND LESBO-IDENTIFIED POLITICAL ANALYSIS, AND IDENTIFY AS BELONGING TO THE FEMINIST MOVEMENT, WHERE LESBIANS HAVE ALWAYS BEEN AT THE FOREFRONT. THEY ALSO DECLARE THEMSELVES AUTONOMOUS, SINCE MALE AND HETEROSEXUAL DOMINATION PERMEATES ALL THE INSTITUTIONS OF CIVIL SOCIETY, WHETHER STATE OR PRIVATE; THEY SEEK TO ENSURE THEIR FREEDOM OF THOUGHT AND PRAXIS, AND TO CONTRIBUTE TO THE CONSTRUCTION OF NEW PROPOSALS FOR CIVILISATION[42].

42. http://encontropaulistadelesbofeminismo.noblogs.org/

A Milpa is a farming system used in some territories of Abya Yala. Based on ancient agricultural methods, milpa farming produces maize, beans and squash, grown in a concentric circle where each plant provides protection and nutrients to the others. A Milpa is both the physical space, the land, and the plant species that grow on it. A Milpa is also a reflection of the knowledge, technologies and practices necessary to obtain food from the land and work. To "Milpa" means to carry out the whole process, from the selection of the land to the harvest. The concept of the milpa goes beyond a mere system of agriculture, as it involves complex interactions and relationships between people, as well as different relationships with both the plants and the land.

We also know that in 2036, when the first attempt to connect to the Mycorrhiza Intranet took place, the first members of this group died immediately due to the effect of an unknown molecule. And in 2037, when the first successful connection was made, it was after a group of human agents accepted the Less Human Than Human *protocol. This protocol stipulated that an IV of chlorophyll was the first step towards a connection with Intranet Mycorrhiza.*

This text needs 27 plant species in order to be written. This text expresses deep doubts about any concept that begins with "self", including that of "self-experimentation" used by us ourselves. Perhaps it is not about what we make of our lives, but what we do with/in life.

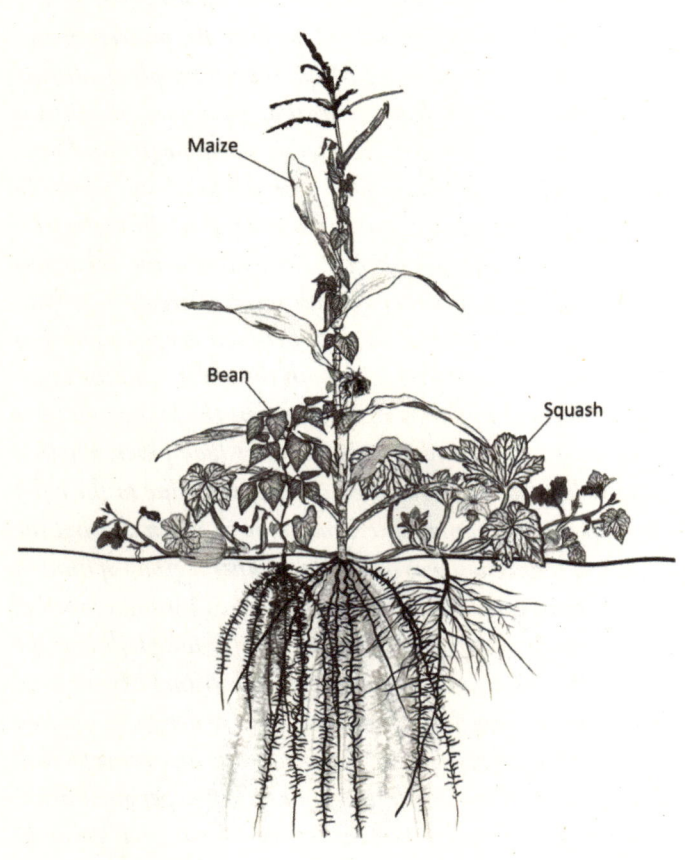

INTERNET FOR BACTERIA

Natalia Rivera
Mutante, Red Suratómica

That nature be a mere resource for humans, now a backward and discarded idea in contemporary thinking, is the idea that continues to underpin the development of emerging digital technologies for communication and exchange. The exploitation of life for these technologies ranges from the internet of things, with an infrastructure that seeks to be ubiquitous, built from the unbridled, colonial, capitalist and ecocidal exploitation of minerals, requiring high levels of energy consumption for supposed economic or relational alternatives such as blockchain, to the latest proposals that saw in living organisms their potential "eco-sustainable" materiality, one that is high-performance and easy to (re) produce, for computing, the cloud and the internet. In the latter case, this refers to the emergence of biocomputing and the possibility of living organisms or molecules derived from living beings being used to store, process and retrieve information relevant to humans, or to create networked computing.

Biocomputing raises the question of how we understand life. Its initial approach is based on thinking of living processes as computational processes, but this idea quickly proves to be very reductionist. This is then countered by the proposal to think of computation and its networks as a living organism. As an alternative, by way of speculative fabulation, a new vision of biocomputers can be proposed, based on more contemporary understandings of life and information[43]: that they are computers that metabolise; metabolising information, which in turn is matter and energy.

Substrates for these biocomputers have included, among others, DNA molecules, proteins, single-celled organisms such as bacteria, and acellular organisms, like the popular mucilaginous mould *Physarum polycephalum*. In the art world, this mould acting as a biocomputer co-composed music with Eduardo Miranda in *Biocomputer Rhythms* (2016)[44], and a fellow fungal com-

43. Maldonado, C. (2022) *Five Arguments toward Understanding Life in Light of a Physics of the Immaterial.* Proceedings 2022, 81, 19. https://doi.org/10.3390/proceedings2022081019

44. Miranda, E. (2016) *Biocomputer Rhythms* [Biocomputer and musical performance]. http://neuromusic.soc.plymouth.ac.uk

panion communicated via electrical signals with humans in an interspecies communication booth with *Myconnect* (2013)[45] by Saša Spačal, Mirjan Švagelj, Anil Podgornik, and Tadej Droljc.

Bacteria, for their part, form the perfect setting for the exploration of these new ways of computing, or co-metabolising, with the living. As Ben-Jacob[46] proposed in 2009 as part of his beautiful idea to transform the way we understand the processes of living beings: we can learn about natural information processing from bacteria. Bacteria are now considered to be capable of processing large and complex amounts of information, and even of processing this information within a network, carrying out parallel computing, for example.

With Margulis, we discovered at the end of the last century that those microorganisms we once considered too small to have a significant impact, particularly on human health, in fact possess marvellous ways of inhabiting, existing, knowing, understanding and creating. A bacterium, as she put it, is never just a bacterium, they are in fact huge complex communities engaged in a constant exchange of information (matter and energy). And

45. Spačal, S., Švagelj, M., Podgornik, A., and Droljc,T. (2013) *Myconnect* [Installation]. https://www.agapea.si/en/projects/myconnect

46. Ben-Jacob, E., (2009). *Learning from Bacteria about Natural Information Processing*. In: Ann. N. Y. Acad. Sci. (October), 1178: 78-90.

the biosphere is a great web of interconnected, intracon-
nected bacteria; bacteria as a superorganism[47].

This intraconnection, as understood drawing from
Barad's concepts[48], speaks to the great organism that is
bacteria and how it allows for the emergence of surprising behaviours/phenomena, showing how life, without
paying attention to universal laws, borders, governments,
etc., makes its path, mutating, diversifying and co-con-
stituting its environment, changing its codes. Such is the
case of symbiosis, which can also give way to the emergence of new living organisms - this was one of Margulis'
major ideas: symbiogenesis as one of the ways in which
evolution forges its path[49] –. Or horizontal gene transfer, a process by which bacteria have the ability to share
genetic information with other bacteria, without being
their progenitors. With this bacterial technology, each
cell has access to a huge gene pool, from which they can
constantly learn new behaviours. Like resistance to anti-
biotics, for example.

We will talk a little more about horizontal gene transfer in this text, as it is this process that can usually met-
aphorically be referred to as the "internet of bacteria",

47. Margulis, L. & Sagan, D. (1995) *Microcosmos. Four Billion Years of Microbial Evolution.* University of California Press.

48. Barad, K. (2007). Meeting the universe halfway. Quantum Physics
and the Entanglement of Matter and Meaning. Duke University Press.

49. Margulis, L. (1999) *Symbiotic Planet: A New Look at Evolution.* Basic
Books.

and it is this process that, in conjunction with synthetic biology, is what is proposed to help create the internet of bacteria, as part of the internet of bio-nano things (IoBNT). This version of the internet of things seeks to use bacteria as materiality, which in this context refers to the concept of "things", i.e. sensors, processors and actuators, computers connected to the cloud.

Considering their simplicity, given cells consist only of a cell membrane and the DNA inside of it, bacteria have developed impressive living technologies to make their way. A large part of their ability to resist, multiply and diversify lies in the fact that they can very easily mutate their genetic code, for example, to appropriate new fragments and use them immediately. This is what happens through horizontal gene transfer. In a typical environment that allows for this, bacteria can release pieces of DNA that remain for a certain period of time until they are captured by other bacteria, even from other species. Alternatively, when they come into contact with each other, the membranes of bacteria allow for the movement of pieces of DNA from one to the other, as part of plasmids, which are DNA molecules outside chromosomal DNA.

Finally, another possibility for horizontal gene transfer is a living technology, which is in itself a beautiful hack to the technologies of another life form. In this process, a very common type of virus called bacteriophage, i.e. a "bacteria eater", turns out to be an unintentional carrier of bacterial information. In one of its usual behaviours, the virus implants its genetic material into a bacterial cell, which, once metabolised by the bacterium, causes the bacterium to reproduce multiple copies of the virus within itself, until due to the pressure differential, they escape and the cell is destroyed. But sometimes, in the reproduction of these copies of the virus, it is not the DNA of the virus that is implanted, but a fragment of the bacterium's DNA. Thus, when this "defective" copy - an interliving entity - of the virus infects another bacterium, it shares bacterial information with it, which can be adapted by the bacterium itself.

This complex, mutant and living network of intraconnections of bacteria, which allows them to share information (which is in turn their knowledge, their life experience), is global and, much to the envy of humans, more than just being decentralised, is distributed, which means it can also be considered their communication system. That is why we imagine it to be their internet. It is this wonderful network - to use it to our advantage, that is, to exploit it - to which we as humans seek to connect our version of the internet of bacteria; and it is here that the narratives informing our approach and the ways in which we develop these technologies of connecting living interentities can be re-thought and re-created from the *undisciplinarity* of a biocentric understanding of the arts and sciences, and not from this normal science (Kuhn)[50], which is controlling and capitalist.

50. Kuhn, T. (2006). La Estructura de las Revoluciones Científicas. Economic Culture Fund, Mexico.

From the perspective of the development of internet of bacteria biotechnology in academia and industry, the implementation of bacteria in the internet of things is not understood as this connection to its ecosystem as just described. In a very different way, developments are proposed that use these microorganisms to perform human processes more efficiently. It is suggested that we humans send information to the bacteria through the cloud so that they act as biosensors, providing information about their environment, or as actuators, executing certain tasks that could be useful for bioremediation or medical treatments, for example9. The networking of bacteria is, on the other hand, considered one of the biggest difficulties for the development of this technology, as sending information to some bacteria would mean that many others could have access to it. This makes them - for all the better - uncontrollable.

On the internet of bacteria, humans decide what information they want to send to bacteria. This information would be sent through the cloud and could, for example, be synthetically generated to be included in a bacterium with motility. This modified bacterium would in turn carry the information to other bacteria in its communities and a certain action determined by humans could be executed10.

Synthetic biology is the enabler of a connection, between more than interspecies, intraliving entities, like this one. Here it becomes the gateway to connect biological and digital living entities. These are biotechnologies with which we humans have been able to replicate other technologies of living organisms, such as gene reproduction, in this specific case. Through synthetic biology, we can produce DNA molecules, which being written digitally can be converted into biological information through a print-like process in a so-called synthesiser.

We in turn have the possibility to read, easily, one could say, biological information such as DNA and convert it into digital information. Through a sequencer, the nitrogenous bases of a DNA molecule are read one by one to become a code containing a sequence, usually very long, consisting of the letters "A, C, G, T". With processes like this, we can gauge the biodiversity of bacteria present in a sample of soil or water, for example, by directly reading their genetic code.

With these two possibilities in mind, those of sequencing and synthesising DNA, I would like to propose a new/ other way of relating, of creating, this emerging medium, that moves radically away from the anthropocentric stance that is currently driving it, towards a biocentric fabulation of bacteria connected to the internet. That the internet of bacteria move from being a technology that seeks to use them as material support, to a technology that enables the emergence of Hyperconnected Bacteria, working as a hybrid organism with which we co-create.

It is about creating an internet FOR bacteria. That all this infrastructure drawn up for the functioning of the other version, the 5G networks, the cloud, the servers that support it, the computers, the sequencers and synthesisers become means for other living organisms. That we share with other living organisms our technological developments just, like their technologies co-constitute us, shape us or are shared with us.

Thus, the radical difference lies in the autonomy of bacteria to share information generated and released by them to their environment, without the intervention of humans. In the internet for bacteria, information in DNA fragments would be released to the environment by bacteria. That DNA would be sequenced to be converted into digital information, the letters ACGT, a code that through the cloud could be quickly retrieved elsewhere in the world and converted, through a synthesiser, into biological information. That is, that code would be re-created as DNA and released into the environment where it can be trapped and adapted by other bacteria. Unlike how it happens conventionally, which is at the local level, horizontal gene transfer through our internet of things infrastructure would allow bacteria to carry out this process between very distant communities.

This proposal arises from thinking about transforming the scientific and developmentalist narratives that usually surround this type of technological creation, which in turn have a strong constitutive power in shaping reality. It is about creating with possibilities as raw material for other worlds, other existences, other forms of life, and not, I wish to state clearly, about a futuristic outlook that pretends to be a solution for various "problems", to further immerse ourselves in the development of digital techno-logical means that are based on massive ecocide processes. What I mean is that it is not "necessary" - as it is usually assumed - to develop this new medium, but that if we do so, it should be from the perspective of what is living, of trusting in life that, by hybridising, is forging its path.

Now, if we return to the perspectives mentioned at the beginning, in which rather than seeing living organisms as computers, we instead understand the process of hybrid-isation of biological and digital systems as biocomputers that metabolise, what emerges from this intraconnection between bacteria and the internet is no longer the use of a human technological medium by other organisms, but instead a new living organism. A bio-digital hybrid organism, a strange and indeterminate form of life with which we co-create, co-metabolise and co-evolve. It is the symbiogenesis of Hyperconnected Bacteria, in which the biosphere is a biodigital superorganism.

With this biocentric understanding of an internet that ceases to be "of" bacteria and becomes an internet "for" bacteria, the deep-seated fear that these microor-ganisms become uncontrollable, or that the exchange of information result in ecological disaster, disappear. This is because it is no longer a question of human interven-tion in the ecosystem, but of a much larger process, that of the hybridisation of organic and inorganic life, of the diversification of life itself. In my view, it is a life-enabling co-creation with that nature of which we are a part, as the living organism that we are. One more way in which life could find its way through humans.

It is in this context, between speculative fabulation[51] and the development of a biotechnology as such, from which the project Hyperconnected Bacteria arises, where together with Mutante, in connection with Red Suratómica, we are exploring the emergence of this strange form of life. It is an undisciplinary project that proposes, just like Marta de Menezes in her project La luna de la Luna (The Moon of the Moon)[52], that a body of research for the development of an almost impossible artistic object be presented as an artistic project. In it we will continue to develop biosensors and interconnection prototypes, for example, while co-creating other fabulations together with scientists, artists, researchers, other creatives and self-organised local communities.

I would like to make a final note on the expression "technologies of the living"[53] that runs through this text.

---

51. Haraway, D. (2019) *Staying with the trouble. Making Kin in the Chthulucene* (Spanish edition). Ed. Consonni.

52. De Menezes, M. (2021) Moon-light (or Moon's Moon). [Skyart] https://martademenezes.com/art/spaces/moon-light-or-moons-moon/

53. We shared this proposal in development with Juan Diego Rivera, Daniela Brill Estrada and Carlos Acosta during the talk *Collaboration and other technologies of the living* (2020), or in the XIV Meeting of Creation - Art and Science (2023) with this concept as a title: Rivera, J.D., Rivera, N.,

It refers to an exploration we at Red Surátomica are carrying out regarding new/other understandings of living beings, in which we consider that the ways in which they process/metabolise information, matter and energy, and the ways in which living beings create and forge their way, can be understood as technologies. Photosynthesis, nitrogen fixation in soils, fungal spores, iridescence in various species, cell mitosis, magnetoreception, mycelial networks, collaboration between human beings, and an infinite number of others. In other words, technologies that make life possible. These understandings have in turn allowed us to understand that, for example, we can stop thinking of the technological as external to living organisms, or that technologies developed by humans, including digital ones, are clearly not as extraordinary as the overwhelming anthropocentrism in which we find ourselves suggests[54].

Brill, D. and Acosta, C. (2020) *Collaboration and other technologies of the living* [Video]. Nexxo Collective. Facebook. https://www.facebook.com/watch/live/?ref=search&v=786080958775880 Red Surátomica (2023). *Technologies of the living.* XIV *Meeting of Creation - Art and Science* [Video]. Surátomica Espacio. Youtube. https://www.youtube.com/watch?v=-0FR_47kb06Y

54. This project is presented by Natalia Rivera, co-created with Mutante and connected to the Suratómica Network, in the context of the II cycle *on the edge of chaos* and the New Media Class Master's Degree at the University of the Arts Berlin UDK.

WHAT DO CLOUDS SMELL LIKE?

Pablo Selín and Lucía Egaña Rojas

> *I get the impression that our culture is full of*
> *absurd ideas, held with unwavering faith by*
> *scientists and everyone else, and that some of these*
> *even void our possible interest in the Earth.*
> Lynn Margulis

1- An omnipresent gas

The internet is a ubiquitous gas.

The internet has transformed into a gas, an additional oxygen from which to obtain confirmation of others' existence. To become a gas, it was necessary to become colourless and odourless, to transform and abstract itself. To become ubiquitous, it was necessary for the material of the internet to become invisible.

This process of becoming invisible, ubiquitous and immediate, has been the product of collective efforts with very different and often opposing motivations. It has made use of research, personal, collective and corporate projects, ideas, war, death, theft, obsession, performance and time. But if for a majority of people, the material reality of the internet behaves like an invisible and absolute gas, for those who work with it, the internet is something else. It is, if anything, a condensed gas, a material reality with which they work, and also a declarative reality, in which the bridges or distribution pipes of this gas are built. The gas has had to condense somewhere.

The clouds in this grid are not made of water, but of the gas that sometimes becomes visible at its dew point. From our phones we have access to a small supply of this gas, a constant but minuscule flow and therefore invisible, odourless, discreet. This is the data the user of the device is interested in.

The condensed gas is the technical and physical space (metallic, silica and polymers). The cloud, the gas reservoir, is such an informationally dense space that explaining all the variables that come into play makes you dizzy. Such are the preliminary symptoms of gas intoxication.

There is a lot of talk about information travelling. But the internet today, rather than showing a journey, seems to show absolute and ubiquitous presence. Is there a journey in that microsecond it takes for every optimised text message, every word that reaches you, that moment when you snoop on the other person *writing*... Can something be a journey if it takes less than a blink of an eye to appear in front of your eyes?

It is the quest for ubiquity on behalf of those who create information technologies, that has rendered the energy burned in each and every query invisible, in each request or data submission (a text message, a social media post, a website visit, a map). The need for immediacy covers up the heat and pollution of server farms, the fatigue of content checkers (often located in less economically privileged or low-income countries).

The diversification and professionalisation of the world wide web has abstracted the materiality of its parts. The original physical device (the server) has gradually disappeared to give way to services in which the original machine (the computer in charge of transferring data and carrying out operations) is fragmented into multiple machines, each optimised for a different function. The idea of the server, or a set of servers, is no longer sufficient to understand what the internet has become, what was once a server has disintegrated into the idea that everything is a service[55], a process or a statement in

---

55. It's a matter of opening your browser and looking for "as a service" types, any word or phrase ending in "aas" (Paas, Saas, and so on) that offer things that used to be a well-defined object as an abstraction of components and processes quantifiable as a monthly cost. It is also familiar IT jargon for "serverless" network infrastructure systems, which imply, in a very simplified form, that your data and processes are spread opportunisti-

code that is born, dies, and sometimes reproduces itself. Everything has become words, utterances in computer languages of many kinds. Everything has become a service, a service without physicality turned into a monetisation system. Ultimately, materiality is completely hidden and becomes just a series of statements, of requests where the last thing you know is how much you are going to spend[56]. A system of abstract quantification, without a material correlate, or perhaps, a system that installed its materiality in a form of mining that works through digital processes. A mining of electricity that runs in parallel with the literal extraction of minerals in the most convenient conditions possible for corporations. The convenience being that of taking advantage of a difference in economic, labour and human rights conditions around the world. If I am a global technology company, that means considering these factors and gauging to what extent I can grow by exploiting inequalities within an unevenly functioning globalisation. Growing by exploiting the inequality of speeds: while economic transactions and imports/exports move quickly, consensus on labour, migration and human rights takes much longer, or in some cases is never made at all.

cally across different locations and systems as appropriate, but never have a single physical address.

56. The YAML configuration language, standard in cloud services, is basically a series of declarations, a language that just says "I want these things laid out in this way" and "I have these tokens" - these are the keys that show that I'm paying for the things I'm asking for.

Web development and its peripheral disciplines have, in their quest for immediacy and efficiency, obfuscated, perhaps on purpose, perhaps as a side effect, the reality of the physical elements that provide connection, and ultimately the visibility of digital information that is being accessed. It is probably similar to what happens with almost everything: it is difficult to dress oneself, feed oneself or carry out any activity that has not passed through one of these global production chains. Why should the internet be any different? Its utopian and democratic discourse is slowly crumbling[57], but that doesn't seem to be reason enough for us to stop using it.

The server, understood as a physical machine parked in some data centre[58], has become an unusual reality. Websites and applications are now usually hosted on virtual servers, with each of their processes abstracted in containers that run only the minimum of each process, anonymously, partially and quantifiable down to the sec-

---

57. It is interesting that a company like Google previously opened its code of conduct with the phrase "Don't be evil", as a statement of intent that gradually stopped being used, apparently following a lawsuit by some of its programmers who felt that by working for US Immigration Services they were not really respecting the statute. Part of the story can be found at https://en.wikipedia.org/wiki/Don%27t_be_evil.

58. Data centres are formally buildings or infrastructures where a number of computers, servers and ultimately data are housed. Much of the information on the internet is data stored in a data centre somewhere in the world.

ond[59]. The aim is not sustainability, but optimisation and speed of response, ubiquity and "gasification". The aim is to optimise in order to spend less money, not less energy. It is the capitalist undercurrent exploring how the least resources can be used to obtain the greatest profit. To make a play on the words of Shakira, creating a Rolex with a Casio investment.

Things have become very complicated. But also, "websites" are no longer so prominent. Most of the data traffic is on streaming systems and hyper-targeted advertising platforms like ~~Facebook~~, ~~Instagram~~ or ~~TikTok~~. Nobody stores music on their devices anymore, everything is listened to or watched online. Our cultural and social habits mean huge digital traffic, which allows our paths and preferences to be accurately tracked. Being permanently connected allows us to control our "consumption" of information. It is no longer an "access point" but a permanent supply, an infinite scroll, an episode that plays automatically after the previous one. How are you going to get on the internet if you spend all your time already on it? And what is the invisible cost of this investment

---

59. AWS or Amazon Web Services has a calculator where you can calculate every operation of your digital project for each second you will use each resource. The problem is that the calculator is so specific and complex that it is quite esoteric for anyone who is not familiar with the specific jargon that Amazon uses to define its IT components. Ultimately they are the ones who have the formula to bill for every single second of IT support you require from them.

beyond the flat rate for your phone bill or the Wifi connection at home?[60]

2- Metal clouds

It was precisely condensation that was the subject of the first visions of clouds. The scientist Gaston Tissandier focused much of his attention on fog, describing it as an ocean of condensed air and ice. Although sparking some interest, scientists had not yet begun to name the phenomenon. After the advent of aviation, they sought to better understand atmospheric behaviours that accompanied the presence of clouds. It was the image that appeared in space, that could be seen beyond the window and that, in their zeal to dominate territory, they wanted to be able to map.

The sky was becoming loaded with representations of it, it seemed like a space full of mythology which, however, was rationalised through photography, especially after the Second World War. The war brought more "scientific", radioactive representations, linked to research into death.

By the mid-twentieth century, representation of clouds dealt with the topic of death. Nuclear tests were

60. Between 2014 and 2016 I had to work with a mobile internet connection that limited my data consumption and, in order to be able to work throughout the month without having to buy more data, I calculated that a day's work as a web developer cost me (at that time) between 700 and 1600 MB (between consulting documentation, uploading and downloading code to the web and coordinating meetings via chat and voice calls).

photographed, and later representation of atomic bombs in Japan created an imaginary that merged cloud and smoke. The idea of the 'toxic cloud' spread. Technological imaginaries have recorded the tools of war in great detail, generating a field of study and also a genre of cultural representation, such as war science fiction.

Cloud computing, on the other hand, is a physical (but sometimes also gaseous), dense infrastructure made of metal, concrete, water and cables. It is an infrastructure that generates heat, and has to be kept cool in order not to collapse. It is also a network of interacting computer systems. It is different languages talking to each other, accepting and rejecting each other according to their own definition. Unlike the clouds in the sky, computer clouds belong to individuals, to companies, to governments.

The concept of the cloud may have begun as a marketing concept to promote the skyward ascent of your own data, as opposed to the physical infrastructures that had been used to store information, the idea of the cloud offers an abstract space in which to house your digital content. The discourse of constant and secure backup in abstract, tested and vaporous infrastructures versus your own machine, your pendrive, your external hard drive, has been hitched up to another sanitised, dematerialised mechanic framework, moving away from the imaginary of iron, smoke and steam that had characterised machines since the Industrial Revolution. More steam and less punk.

So, after years of uploading our data to the cloud, we realised that these clouds had always been private property, a glass capsule shut with multiple locks and passwords. A closed system with small opening gates from which your data and processes exit.

The cloud is a network, a web of physical components (servers, computational units, objects with an internet connection) and a network of processes and statements through which different types of functionality (chat, streaming, calls, websites, bank accounts) are obtained. The cloud is not just a data bank, it is above all a "distributed unit". It is the fragmentation of an operation in different places, having consequences at all the points from which it is called. It is a self-repairing network, always offering 99.99% availability, as a weapon designed to withstand any bombardment, because it is distributed all over the world.

The concept of the cloud appeared in computer science in 1990 as a result of research that had been carried out since the 1960s on the ARPANET network[61], created by the US Department of Defence to send military data and connect research centres housed in US universities. It was intended primarily for war, to build a resilient computer network, which would find all possible ways for data to travel, to survive the paranoid scenarios imagined during the Cold War.

It is this resilient cloud, this infectious cloud, that has enabled the latest stage of late-stage capitalism, and has

61. Advanced Research Projects Agency Network.

accelerated the creation of more and more clouds of CO_2. It has facilitated instant transactions, production chain distribution and cultural standardisation. This cloud is virtual, and yet it contributes to making summers more dangerous every year for many human and non-human animals[62].

3- A pluriversal cloud

If the internet is a gas that is among us, a second breath, that implies that, as with oxygen, butane or any other gas, there is a space of emission or production of this material. The "condensation space", the reservoir where the pressure is higher and you can feel the weight and fluctuation of the gaseous material.

What http://pluriversidadnomada.net[63] has tried to do is find these points of condensation where certain aspects of the materiality of the internet can be appreciated. To find and undress points of expenditure and its functionality (energetic and symbolic). A website that can explain how it works and what is happening in its traffic flows, so that you can truly see what you're looking at. We have sought to create an educational website.

62. On environmental violence and toxic clouds, see the article *"Ver las nubes. Estudio sobre las formas de representación de las nubes tóxicas y su impacto en los modos de ver las violencias"* by Melissa Valenzuela Gómez at: http://revistaindex.net/index.php/cav/article/view/476/460

63. Pablo Selin is the programmer in charge of the Pluriversidad Nómada website, this text has been nourished by a series of conversations and work processes held in that context.

A website that is a working tool. A website that can be accessed from different places and from different digital conditions, different devices, systems and internet speeds. This was the starting point for the development of the Pluriversidad Nómada website.

The aim was to build a digital space in which the content would play with its presentation, but at the same time serve the practical purposes of the pedagogical project. A utilitarian tool but one that would give an account of what was happening on each visit.

The programming work began during the creation of Pluriversity, and its structure had to respond to the way in which the project was configured, seeking to provide organisation and flexibility to the different sections of the site, which could enter into relationships between its different Institutes and additional classification systems, and which could also be a site that possible of being quickly constructed, and whose contents could be modified by people with different digital capacities.

To achieve this, we worked with tools that have been used and tested for several years on the web, that have open licences and are available for modification and reuse, that have a community of developers and documentation, so that results are freely available and can be replicated, reused or recycled in the future[64].

64. For content management, a template was created from scratch with WordPress, and Javascript was used for the energy expenditure systems and

We also sought to create a system that would allow toggling between a "high energy" and a "low energy" version that would consider factors that might most affect a visitor with reduced bandwidth, and also which systems could be removed from the site, keeping it functional but with less energy and computational expenditure[65]. During the development of this tool, additional components around data and information traffic on the internet focussed on, and have been incorporated into different sections of the project and are being released as code tools that can be reused and analysed by others.

An energy expenditure calculator has also been created for the website, which uses data from an open platform for calculating CO_2 consumption, and combines it with the amount of data generated and processed by the Pluriversidad Nómada website to make an estimate that is expressed in daily activities that basically "translate" this unitary visit to the website. In turn, each of these unitary visits are added to a global register of visits that create ways of visualising the total and collective expenditure of maintaining the information on this website online.

On a material level, the physicality of Nomadic Pluriversity's data is hosted on a low-cost, high-availa-

the relationship map. The code is available in Pluriversidad Nómada's Github repository (https://github.com/pabloselin/pluri_web).

65. For the low-power version, most of the Javascript code, additional fonts, images and stylesheets were removed.

bility, carbon-neutral shared server, which, contrary to what one might imagine, is located in one of the territories that generates the most CO_2: The United States. The Nomadic Pluriversity site and applications inhabit a shared space with other websites on a "traditional" server in the sense that its processes, costs and digital operations impact on all its neighbours and, likewise, the processes of the neighbourhood of sites can affect the stability of the Nomadic Pluriversity site[66].

This hosting decision, somewhere between pragmatism and a statement of intent, has allowed the project to offer a promise of compatibility in the future. There is also little certainty about what the internet will become in the coming years, with the imposition of new standards that seek to force the consumption of advertising[67] and

66. The traditional structure of "shared hosting" implies that you share the physical space of a computer, with its available memory, processor and storage, with different levels of precaution so that your neighbours or fellow servers cannot take up all the data or all the resources, but a shared server, unlike the virtualised environments that are becoming the norm these days, still runs the risk that a process will run amok and crash the server. A bit like when the bathtub in the upstairs neighbour's house fills up and floods all the floors below.

67. The "Web Integrity API" proposed by Google is basically a DRM (digital rights management) for websites, which would make it impossible to view certain websites depending on what kind of device you use, or what kind of extensions you have installed, making it practically impossible to block advertising. More info at: https://github.com/RupertBenWiser/Web-Environment-Integrity/tree/main

walled gardens of content[68], which is where most of digital activity seems to be moving. We have not yet estimated the cost of the digital presence of Nomadic Pluriversity beyond its website, how much has been spent on its (our) emails, its Instagram™ posts, Telegram™ and Whatsapp™ chats, videoconferences on Jitsi™, Skype™ or Zoom™.

The work at Nomadic Pluriversity to develop a narrative on energy consumption is just beginning, with preliminary explorations of carbon expenditure we have been able to make a comparison with domestic activities. We are interested in being able to "ground" the material implications in an everyday life that is made up of meals, exercise, travel and transport. To bring the clouds down to earth.

We want the virtual space of the cloud to be as tactile as possible, to be able to pass through the cloud and become aware of its temperature, its density. Only by traversing the cloud will we be able to find the free and common spaces that still remain. To go through it we must first be able to see it, hopefully touch it, feel how the gas gets into our lungs and, by smelling it, see what we can do with it.

68. This refers to services that are inaccessible to users and, as the garden analogy suggests, only allow entry and exit at the points designed for that purpose, as well as access to the "species" (e.g. software) that have been made available by default or in the initial manufacturing configuration, without much possibility of altering these configurations.

LENGUARACES OF THE FUTURE, BREEDING RUINS FOR OUR VISIONARY CHAOS

val flores

A pedagogical practice is an imaginative practice. An imaginative practice needs a language to make it exist. A language is an archive of futures that becomes the present as a practice of the past. An archive is a material translation of time. Time is a visionary ruin.

A pedagogical practice is an artistic practice: devices of self-alteration of life, exercises of collective creation, aimed at activating unusual experiences of knowledge construction and ways of relationship with the living and nonliving world. It becomes a tentative rehearsal of creative and investigative processes to explore the affective contingencies of our plural existence. It envisions the collective as a system for projecting ideas, the body as a working method, the word as artistic and political material, thought as aesthetics. To make other ways of life possible, languages and imagination are the experimental and inventive conditions of a pedagogical frequency.

An imaginative pedagogical practice must be willing to disorganise one's own (non) knowledge. To devise liminal situations as zones of contagion and cross-border contamination where life and education, the ethical condition and aesthetic creation intersect, and where pedagogical traditions, subjective intensities, performance, visual arts, forms of activism, and forgotten memories intermingle. A cuir/queer wandering, winding through what is unforeseen, unexpected, improvised and surprising. This act of wandering decolonises, as an unprecedented event, as an uncertain becoming, a word that can be touched, a new seditious sensibility. This wandering devises an ecopoetics that is timeless, open to the dispersion of any minimal gesture that varies material in the environment. Ideating in tandem with Gloria Anzaldúa and her epistemology of the imagination[69], as an interrogation and affectation of the paradigms that govern hegemonic notions of reality, identity, creativity, activism, spirituality, race, gender, class and sexuality.

---

69. Anzaldúa, Gloria (2021) "Preface. Gestures of the body – escribiendo para idear". *Light in the Dark. Rewriting Identity, Spirituality, Reality* (Spanish edition). Translation: Valeria Kierbel and Violeta Benialgo. Buenos Aires: Hekht.

***

A pedagogical practice tests out a language to name what is done. A language offers a way of thinking. A language expresses affection. A pedagogical practice exercises a politics of naming that creates different everyday relations with the living. It is an erotic practice, and also an erratic one, an art of inaccuracy where we have no choice but to coexist amidst tensions. Because translation is not synonymous with elucidation, it is rather experimenting with misunderstandings. It is a relationship with words that is strange and insurgent.

Baptiste Morizot and his group practise tracking, alongside a practice of naming that alters relations with the living world. They rehearse a philosophical stuttering to track an "eco-sensitive" name in their records of practices that place us in a different mood regarding the environment. "Where are we going tomorrow?" they ask. And they try out different versions: "To nature", they say at first. But they dismiss it, because the idea of nature is "a fetish of this civilisation that rightly has a problematic, conflictive and destructive relationship with the living world"[70]. They keep trying: "tomorrow we're going out-

70. Morizot, Baptiste (2020) "Bosquizarse (to forest oneself)". From *On the Animal Trail* (Spanish edition). Translation: Francisco Gelman Constantin. Buenos Aires: Isla Desierta.

side", "tomorrow we're going to the bush", "tomorrow we're going to the open air". Each answer opens up a swarm of questions and inconveniences.

To twist the way of saying is to twist the way of thinking[71]. A word from the Algonquian people in Canada[72] draws close to their experience. "To forest oneself". A word that contains a double movement: we move towards the forest as much as it moves towards us. Naming in this different way creates a different relationship with living territories. One generating a connection through other manners of attention and practices, letting ourselves be colonised by them, letting ourselves be situated, letting them move within us.

It is a matter of collapsing the lexicon of normative pedagogies to promote sexual and ecological creativity. To break with obligatory relationships between words and identities. To tear up the sensitive agreements of

71. flores, val (2018) "Esporas de indisciplina. Pedagogías trastornadas y metodologías queer", in *Pedagogías transgresoras* II. Bocavulvaria Ediciones, Santo Tomé (Santa Fe).

72. When I wrote this essay I used this name following the Spanish translation of Morizot's book. Later, in the process of translating this text into English, translator Stephanie Graham drew my attention to the colonial bias of this name for this people. The Algonquin people of Ontario call themselves omàmiwinini (plural: omàmiwininiwak) or by the more generalised name of anicinàpe (plural: anicinàpek). I am grateful to Stephanie for pointing this out, accounting not only for the proper name, but for those colonial as well as decolonising forces that inhabit our language and that are political contests over the words by which we give ourselves existence.

epistemological asepsis and scriptural hygiene. To maintain an open horizon of possibilities and desirabilities that broaden and multiply imaginaries, and potential versions of them.

This deals with disputes over words that create infringements of educational temporalities. Listening to the coexistence of overlapping and ununified times, dislocated from the tropes of progress and evolution. Diverting teleologies of knowledge that are "forward"-oriented, that "advance". A temporal dislocation where we become seismographers of the echoes of a language that seeks to displace human exceptionality, and consider how we create and co-create our lives, identities and bodies. Keeping open different narratives capable of escaping explanations that present themselves as dominant, unique, universal[73].

Inheriting the trouble in order to rewrite it in a lower-case language, one which has been disavowed by heroic narratives and the vertical, upright, bipedal, frontal ways of taking the floor, that claim transparency and intelligibility in their political, rhetorical and epistemic phrases. In turn, writing in a lower-case language for a

73. Bonilla Sztern, Camila (2019) ¿Es posible un pensamiento más que humano? Notas a partir de la obra de Vinciane Despret para una etología filosófica. Latin American Journal of Critical Animal Studies Year VI, Vol I. June 2019. La Plata: Latin American Institute of Critical Animal Studies. In Memoria Académica. Pp. 19-32.

political imaginary that's as vast as the smallest speck of a mycelial network.

***

And so, this means disobedient and untamed political fictions rising from a lower-case language. Undisciplined and magnetic imaginations that have the sole of their foot in the past and the heel in the future. Marosa di Giorgio and her omens, feeling hope in the past and finding memories in the future. A *prophetic vision of the past* for Édouard Glissant. Inhabiting astonishment as an affective practice on the chiaroscuro spectrum of a forgotten past, be it erased or crushed, in and by a soporific present. Deserting the imperative of novelty and its logic of consumption, spurring a grammar of anxiety and control as the means of governing the soul. Trawling fictions, that create a perceptive disturbance of an erotics of (not) knowing. Discerning what's left, the hangover, what's lost, the residue, the regression, attentional dispositions, inducing sensory practices that interfere with particular orchestrations of time, those whose regimes of power are converted into rhythms and bodily routines.

In order to be a teacher of the invisible, a *sensory worker in the dismantling of language*[74], how can we escape from the pedagogic ways of asking questions that insist on *duty*

74. flores, val (2022) *Labiar el desierto*. Buenos Aires: La Libre.

as political imagination? Duty and desire are not opposed, because there is also a desire for duty, but what would happen if we replace *duty* with *desire*? This question contains a mode of imagination, of the (un)imaginable.

Escaping from moral questions that call for prescriptions or programmes. The "shoulds" try to solve problems with imperative modes that are based on security, certainty, convenience and comfort, thus disregarding the contingencies and accidents of the very occurrence of an action in movement. This speaks to a habitual politic, one that is schooled and militarised. Halting this question as a gesture of inhibitory, but not repressive, thought. Opening up to other directions, forms of attention and possibilities. Invoking the imaginative and desiring libidinal energy of the echoes of this lower-case revolution. Exhuming the rebellious ideals that would brighten the ordinary existence of those who have gone astray. Recovering and recreating the insurgent echo of lives and peoples who tirelessly imagine other ways of living[75].

These are fictions that plunge us into the realm of possibility by challenging the fortuitous limits of what will be considered reality, triggering a process of liberation from restrictions on ways of thinking, writing, creating and

---

75. Hartman, Saidiya (2019) *Wayward lives, beautiful experiments. Intimate histories of social upheaval.* New York, London. W. W. Norton & company. Own translation.

researching, without aligning ourselves with the norms of the bureaucratic exercise of the word.

How can a pedagogical practice be created as an experience of temporary estrangement from, and awakening to, a culture, rather than a gesture of peaceful integration into the politics of knowledge of a time, a body, a sex? [76]

***

future lenguaraces, breeding ruins for our visionary chaos[77]. Testing out and feeling a new political fiction. The sensual practice of figurations as fictional (dis)knowledge. A material experience of thought, going against the consumerist disciplining of a more sensitive practice of the word.

76. This question was part of the workshop-performance "Tiempos perdidos: el retroceso como atracción pedagógica (Lost times: regression as a pedagogical attraction)". At the II Cuir Pedagogical Studies Conference. Trans/disciplines, In/disciplines, and End/disciplines. Organised by: Research Group on Education and Cultural Studies (GIEEC)/ Research Group on Philosophy of Education (GIFE) Centre for Multidisciplinary Research in Education (CIMED)/ Department of Education Sciences/ Faculty of Humanities, UNMdP/ PedagOrgía: Cuir Extension Group. Teatro Auditorium. Mar del Plata, 19 August 2022.

77. *Lenguaraces of the future, breeding ruins for our visionary chaos* was the title of a workshop imagined as a vital and textual game of improvising live acts of writing. A workshop that never took place. It was scheduled with the PEI (Independent Study Programme of the Museum of Contemporary Art of Barcelona), but was cruelly and scandalously cancelled in 2021 by the MACBA administration.

A somatic exercise of poetic imagination that takes on the strength of the "in-between", those passages of thresholds and times. Figurations as an epistemological procedure and poetic tactic that rethink past and possible future scenarios, without being anchored to an evolutionary and positive narrative of thought, making the writings more ambiguous and complex.

> *how do we hear in each word the living remains of a forgotten past and an ignored future? how does the power of ruins act in our writing? what alphabets of destruction make up our creative practices? can ruin be an alchemical act that makes writing an affective practice of future (dis) knowledge? what sensitive and conceptual commitments are involved in cultivating speculative fictions with the remains of the opaque, the imperceptible, the fragile, the untranslatable? how do we make the word pass through our bodies without annihilating the unpredictable languages of the living? where does the asynchronous feast of our desiring vulnerabilities breathe?*

can the practice of questioning be a rehearsal for an unsuspected future?

A future that can be felt in lower case and in the plural as an uncolonised dream. "We cannot build what we cannot imagine", everything that is built was first imagined[78].

Everything that is built was first a question.

This speaks to an art of composing with ruins, with our broken pieces, at the edges of the great normative histories we splinter, interfering with the rhetorics of triumph, of joy, well-being, performance, productivity, as imperatives of neoliberal and neocolonial capitalism.

These ruins exist as oracular contraband, where multiple senses of possibility are trafficked. They are ruins that fall outside the clear-cut models of political narratives. Ruins as reserves of knowledge to be invented or reactivated. Ruins as a practice of babbling and murmuring, that neither possesses nor seeks a clear and transparent articulation. Ruins as temporary compasses that point to other possible sensibilities. Ruins as felt legacies of unrealised futures. Ruins as a tentative space faced with the weary time of the now. Because in the debris of each discipline, of each practice, of each genre, an unsuspected fertility resounds to create other pos-

78. As the co-editors of Octavia Butler's book Xenogenesis, Walidah Imarisha and Adrienne Maree Brown, suggest. Quoted in Jota Mombaça: ¡Rumbo a una re-distribución de la violencia des-obediente de género y anticolonial! Translated by elcinia torres. In *Devuélvannos el oro. Cosmovisiones perversas y acciones anticoloniales*, Colectivo Ayllu. Madrid: Matadero Centro de Residencias Artísticas. 2018

sible lives that are already present in this time or in its epochal undertow, plotting gestures with the repudiated futures of the past.

In this scene of ruin, one state of language is decomposed by means of another. It is a speculative practice of ruining the world that ruins us, of imagining unspectacularising futures, in lowercase, plural, fragile, imperceptible letters, our feet disenchanted and our hands desirous. It is a work of imagination and reverie that learns from the past. Learning from science fiction: the past demands a surprise[79].

The past and surprise. The *lenguaraz*, foul-mouthed, of uncontrolled speech. An impure, bloody, disloyal genealogy. Disloyal to the conquest of America, disloyal to the conquest of the desert in Argentina. *Languaraces*. Interpreters who communicated and confused the white world with the Indigenous world. Undesirable, but fatally indispensable, the *lenguaraces* ruined any pretence of pure and clear interpretation. They were contradictory, ambiguous figures, stuck to betrayal, to the liminal, living between worlds, languages, times.

languaraces of the future does not refer to a specific subject. Not even a human one. An imaginative proce-

79. Butler, Octavia (2000) "Some rules for predicting the future", originally published in Essence magazine [2000] / and reproduced by the editors of exittheapple.com in April 2007. Translation from (((o)))) Acoustic Mirror. @espejoacustico & José Pérez de Lama (2020); the original in English, following the Spanish version.

dure that senses the rumour of a futuristic yearning and resents other worlds in which differences coexist at the level of the creative task. It has premonitions, because it is creating a felt experience based on the intuition that something is going that way, the moving eroticism of touching another time, the palpation of the ecstasy of a kind of geological listening. It resents because it invites us to return to what we have already felt, to perceive it in another way, at the same time it sticks with the pain and anger provoked by inequality and oppression.

languaraces of the future that speak in tongues. Spectral Anzaldúa and her flaming tongues as an alchemical process synthesising dualities, contradictions and perspectives from these different selves and worlds[80]. *breeding ruins for our visionary chaos*. Wittig and Zeig write a draft *vision* for ancestral disorder:

Visions, like hallucinations, are phenomena that lovers develop in a state of sloth. In lazy sacks, on trees, in lazy eggs, in gardens, the lovers fall "prey" to visions. It should be noted that the expression "prey", which indicates an unhappy state, is not the meaning. Here it means memory. Indeed, in times of chaos, people who had visions were said to be "prey to visions". They were considered sick and

80. Anzaldúa, Gloria (1988) Hablar en lenguas. Una carta a escritoras tercermundistas. In Cherrie Moraga and Ana Castillo, *Esta puente, mi espalda. Voices of Third World women in the United States*. ism press. San Francisco.

were often locked up. Lovers in the age of glory give their visions when they are in a state of sloth and availability. The visions of the past make it possible to rescue residues of our history that most of the texts from before the glory age had disfigured. Visions of the past are told from place to place, from community to community, from island to island, from continent to continent, from inhabited forest, from ice floe to ice floe, by the bearers of fables. The visions of the present are communications between lovers who live in distant places. Some lovers give each other appointments of visions. They are the occasion of festivities, of intimate joys. Visions of the future are often incomprehensible, but always joyful[81].

Words and images, animated sepulchres. Remains of a past and visionary ruins of an ignored future. Wandering along these remains, organising rites of resurrection as a pedagogical practice. Harvesting their unexpected, cancelled, annihilated possibilities. To make appointments of visions as an artistic practice.

lenguaraces of the future training the poetic nose to track down the smoke of destruction, of those ruins as the legacy to generate imagination as a decolonising force that frees the world to come, from the trap of the world

81. Wittig, Monique and Sande Zeig (1981) *Lesbian Peoples: Material for a Dictionary* (Spanish edition). Translation: Cristina Peri Rossi. Barcelona: Editorial Lumen.

to end. A wager on the *visionary chaos* that palpitates with the imaginative force of the gestures at hand. Because the first reparation is that of the imagination.

PART II

QUEER ATLAS /
SF: TRANS*PLANT

Ce Quimera

21, 22 and 23 June, 5—9pm
Es Local – Palma de Mallorca – Europe

Our minds are incarcerated by our words. [...] Biology textbooks define "symbiosis" anthropocentrically—as mutually helpful relationships or animal benefits, implying social contract or cost-benefit analysis by the partners. This definition is silly— symbiosis is a widespread biological phenomenon that preceded by eons the human world and the invention of money.

Lynn Margulis from Words as Battle Cries

Reading Lynn Margulis I wonder how to observe, listen, feel, smell in an attempt to generate interspecies bonds without contaminating them with our capitalist and colonialist vision. How do we, as humans, bond with the different, with the strange. I don't think there is a single answer to this, but with these questions as my guide, I try to embark on an ongoing exercise in a dissidence of the senses. An interspecies dissidence.

This workshop was a series of exercises aimed at[82]: laughing, imagining, contradicting ourselves, trying to talk less with our mouths and move our hands more, get-

82. I would like to thank Caro Novella for her non-chronicle of this workshop. Their text in the book tells in a very deep and beautiful way all the processes that took place in three days of coexistence and workshoping. I would also like to give special thanks to La Lioparda Teatre for their warm welcome and love.

ting our fingers covered with agar agar, sliding our breath through our bodies, observing in silence. We were accompanied by the Biodivas healers tarot[83] while we made seed bombs to sow in arid soil.

The name and contents of the workshop transmuted before starting[84]. I kept some lines of research/action that had been raised in Quimera Rosa surrounding the performativity of laboratory life, as well as tools that place the body on the experimental table. Guided by the Trans*Plant project, in this workshop we reflect on self-experimentation and identities beyond gender and kingdom assigned at birth. *Less human than human* and *kingdom dysphoria*[85].

Then we add microscopy and change of scale.

Zooming in x10 we grow our microbiota in petri dishes and incubate them, practising a type of reproduction that isn't human. Bacterial sex: transferring information from one body to another.

Zooming in x40 we set off in search of little bugs who are invisible to the human eye, who inhabit every object,

83. Biodivas Tarot: https://static.wixstatic.com/ugd/57e69f_20d03a13c-c564a24810b052a2a622e57.pdf

84. The initial programme was a workshop by Quimera Rosa (Kina Madno and Ce Quimera) called "SF Trans*Plant: Theoretical and practical introduction to bio-hacking through the chimeric mirror". Finally, I gave the workshop on my own and changed part of its contents and dynamics, orienting it towards themes that I'm investigating outside the collective.

85. For more information about Trans*Plant and Quimera Rosa workshops visit: https://quimerarosa.net/transplant/

every corner of the territory. We look at them under the microscope, concentrating on observing while disobeying: the game is to have fun while studying how biology insists on classifying and taxonomising bodies and relationships; using drawings and photos with an aesthetic that strongly collaborates in putting every form of life in the little box that it corresponds to. These are the same taxonomies that laid the foundations of racism, and all cultural forms of domination of white humans over other humans, and humans over other living beings.

Zooming in x100 is where the Cuir/Queer Atlas comes in, and at this point we lay down on the floor to meditate, draw and write. And I keep collecting, workshop after workshop, numerous new beings that will soon form a great unclassifiable, dirty, disparate, baroque, strange, and delirious Atlas. The Cuir/Queer Atlas is an exercise in invention, in bastardising biological classifications, inspired above all by the work of Lynn Margulis, and not only hers[86], as it is also an exercise in unlearning human corporeality and inhabiting another body, that of a strange bug. We are transported, the environment is liquid humidity where we meet other microscopic beings, and where we perceive the changes of scale to leave, in a way, humanity and words for a while.

86. This Atlas was also nourished by exchanges with Gaia Leandra and Caro Novella.

QUEER ATLAS.
A WORKSHOP STRADDLING
THE CROSSROADS

Caro Novella Centellas

> *It matters what stories tell stories.*
> *It matters what thoughts think thoughts.*
> *It matters what worlds world worlds.*
> Margaret Strathern, via Donna Harraway

Networks - crossroads - workshops

Remember: We don't know what a ~~body~~[87] workshop can do. Nor do we know where or when it begins or ends[88]. What worlds is it comprised of, making it coherent[89]?

---

87. From Spinoza, via Deleuze. Deleuze, Gilles. 1988. Spinoza: Practical Philosophy. San Francisco: City Lights Books.

88. Haraway, Donna J. 1991. "A Manifesto for Cyborgs. Science Technology and Socialist Feminism in the 1980s." In Simians, Cyborgs and Women: The Reinvention of Nature, 150. New York: Routledge.

89. Mol, Anne-Marie. 2016. "Clafoutis as a Composite: On Hanging Together Felicitously." In Modes of Knowing: Resources from the Baroque, 242-65. UK: Mattering Press.

What stories nourish it? What institutions and conceptual genealogies recognise it? What affections enliven it? Through what logic and world views is it imagined? What practices does it employ? What energies, what memories, what other workshops are generated from it? What circuits of knowledge does it interrupt/enlarge? What wisdom is created in the relational landscape of a workshop? What limits, classifications and bodies does it produce?

IMAGES FROM THE WORKSHOP CUIR ATLAS / *SF:TRANS*PLANT* LED BY CE QUIMERA. PHOTO: CARO NOVELLA.

This text was born from Ce Quimera's invitation to use their art and science workshop as the inspiration to write: a sort of nomadic pedagogical imprint, perhaps. I find myself composing it piece by piece while sitting on the porch sofa at Ponderosa - a space inhabited by other genealogies of dance and corporal experimentation - drawing from memory, and the photos and notes I took during the workshop. I wonder about crossovers between Ce's workshop and the ones I'm taking here, on practices that co-compose genealogies and possible worlds. I write with the wish to extend my friend and her offerings beyond here and now. And although this exercise has its antecedents in another text[90], writing this one feels harder. I sense the weight of responsibility for its transmission and impact.

7/09/2023/Revision 4.0- ABSTRACT

Loose record of the workshop Cuir/Queer Atlas – SF:Tran*Plant led by Ce Quimera, organised by Pluriversidad Nómada together with La Lioparda Teatre at Es Local, Mallorca, in June 2023.

ASSISTANTS: L. R. M. O. C. Mi. (et al.)

OBJECTIVE(S): Put into practice models that de-centre the logics of the possessive individual. Blur the boundaries between realms. Share tools and practices. Contaminate

---

90. Text from the workshop "Trans*plant: My Illness is an Artistic Creation" offered by Quimera Rosa in 2018. https://quimerarosa.net/transplant/my-disease-is-an-artistic-creation/ English

science. Collectivise art. Self-experiment. Become experts. Get tangled in the tangled web we weave[91]. Mutate.

METHODOLOGY: Participatory [endosymbiosis] [community science] [self-experimentation] [inoculate] [cultivate ecosystems] [involute] [devolve] [felt experiments] [test] [meditate] [card readings] [holobiont] [cuiring/queering taxonomies].

NOTE TO READER: The pronouns in the text vary. This is deliberate. A few utterances from the lab have been quoted verbatim and are included in italics, sometimes naming the speaker, and sometimes just citing the person's initials (because I didn't ask permission to name them). Sometimes you'll be challenged, and the text often becomes a 3rd-person narrative. The footnotes include references to other texts, as well as notes on conversations opened up through the revision of this text.

WARNING: Although this text thinks along the lines of the workshop, it also wanders toward other ones, focusing its attention elsewhere. Do not expect an objective or neutral account. Not even faithful or "truthful"; take it as a partial and situated device (from the places/times and genealogies/relations of power that I embody), one

---

91. To mark the playfulness of the practice, I've used slang, which translated to English isn't as fun.

that plays with inhabiting intersections and materialising worlds that are always present, even when we can't perceive them.

Practices and narratives

It matters which practices enact practices. Post-pornographic practices, as the legacy of cyborg trans-feminism and self-experimentation, enact alternatives to mainstream porn practices. In so doing, these practices extend bodies, subjectivities and pleasures, opening up sexual imaginaries and blurring male/female, and public/private binaries. *It's all about using different tools for the same questions*, says Ce, framing this workshop as an evolution of the concerns and curiosities that they have dealt with and lived for some time now, alongside Kina within the Quimera Rosa collective. This time around, the binaries to be hacked are different: how do we intervene in the taxonomic practices of modern science, how do we create a cuir atlas that blurs the divisions between kingdoms to offer us possibilities of existence that are less stagnant, less binary, more interdependent - exquisitely attentive to the variations of the other parts?[92]

92. As the science philosopher Isabelle Stengers proposes in: Stengers, Isabelle. 2011. *Thinking with Whitehead: A Free and Wild Creation of Concepts*. Harvard University Press.

[endosymbiosis]

Lynn Margullis, an American evolutionary microbiol-ogist, offers us another evolutionary story - one that goes beyond autonomous, competitive individuals - where bacteria and bugs intertwine, become allies, dance about, seduce each other, eat each other without digesting the other's body, forming larger, more complex critters, con-tinuing to coil together, composing cells and organisms that influence the even very development of plant and animal kingdoms. Endosymbiosis recasts evolution as an act of partial cannibalism, or sustained intimacy between strangers: a symbiotic relationship where one bacterium or several bacteria co-compose/integrate into another cell and establish a cooperative union for all. Another word for these endosymbiotic entities is 'holobionts'.

[open source knowledge]

▷ Bring books that inspired the workshop[93].
▷ Share links to track knowledge (avoiding Powerpoints and their watertight knowledge).

93. Some of them, though as Ce says, "clearly not all of them", are: "A Braid of Sacred Grass" by Robin Wall Kimmerer, "Involutionary Momen-tum" by Carla Hustak and Natasha Myers, the journal "Ni Urras ni Ana-rres" from the Trans*Plant project by Quimera Rosa, and "Five Kingdoms: An Illustrated Guide to the Phyla of Life on Earth" by Margulis, Lynn and Michael J. Chapman.

▷ Unveil protocols, formulas, steps or guidelines.
▷ Encourage group problem solving.
▷ Don't give nor assume to know the answer to every question. Surely there are other possibilities we haven't seen yet.
▷ Read quotes from decolonialist scientists who offer Indigenous words and concepts for things invisible to science[94].
▷ Read cards using the Biodiva healers deck[95].

94. This is the quote from biologist Robin Wall Kimmerer: The language scientists speak, however precise, is based on a profound error in grammar, an omission, a grave loss in translation from the native languages of these shores. My first taste of the missing language was the word *Puhpowee* on my tongue. I came across it in a book written by the Anishinaabe ethnobotanist Keewaydinoquay, in a treatise on the traditional uses of fungi by our people. *Puhpowee*, she explained, translates as "the force which causes mushrooms to push up from the Earth overnight". As a biologist, I was stunned that such a word existed. In all its technical vocabulary, Western science has no such term, no words to hold this mystery. You'd think that biologists, of all people, would have words for life. But in scientific language our terminology is used to define the boundaries of our knowing. What lies beyond our grasp remains unnamed. From Kimmerer, Robin Wall. 2013. *Braiding Sweetgrass*. Minneapolis: Milkweed Editions, pg. 61.

95. A deck of 21 cards representing healers, doctors, nurses, health promoters, shamans and midwives whose work has contributed to the wellbeing of their communities, in an exercise to depatriarchalise and collectively decolonise the history of medicine. Project edited by Klau Chinche for Revista Hysteria. Download it at https://hysteria.mx/baraja-de-sanadoras-biodiva/ (various artists 2021)

▷ Make artemisia seed bombs with clay[96].

[prepare the medium]

Go to the second section of the text: *From Consent to Cosense: Rehearsing Ecologies of Exposure within Quimera Rosa's Trans*Plant: My Disease is an Artistic Creation*[97]. Here you'll find in detail how we prepared the medium, in another workshop, at another time.

[Self-experimentation]

Or how to culture bugs that are present in our own bodies.

1. Rub the isotope vigorously over the area of "your" body that piques your curiosity.
2. Gently brush the isotope against the agar-agar medium.
3. Place the petri dish in the incubator.
4. Let it grow for 24 hours (or more).

---

96. Read more about the pharmaceutical industry and artemisia in the newspaper "Ni Urras ni Anarres" as part of the Trans*Plant project by Quimera Rosa at www.quimerarosa/transplant.net.

97. Read it at: https://revistas.udistrital.edu.co/index.php/CORPO/article/download/14234/15592?inline=1 Novella, Caro. 2019. From Consent to Cosense: Rehearsing Ecologies of Exposure within Quimera Rosa's 'Trans*plant: My Disease Is an Artistic Creation'. Corpographies. Estudios Críticos de y desde los cuerpos 6 (Especial Ecologías Afectivas): 134-52. Bogotá: Udistrital Journals.

L. rubs behind their ear, R. scratches their armpit. M. goes for their tear duct. The elbow, the mouth.

I shove the isotope in my pussy, twist it around a bit. It feels wet. *That's where they'll be. Between my toes. You have to get creative*, says M.

[gathering colonies]

We go out seeking wet places. It rained today, yet you can hardly tell; 35°C and it feels like a desert. We look for potential critter paradises. We seem to be guided by disgust: pigeon poo, a slimy thing stuck to a bench, the mouth of a hose, a piece of rotting leaf in the fountain, leftover food. How strange this logic - of life as disgust - is.

[Inoculate]

Taking a small sample we dilute it with a drop of distilled water. This way we thin it out, so we can place the coverslip on top, so a higher magnification lens can be brought closer to the specimen. The method can stress the microorganisms, meaning they might stop moving for a while.

[Look under the microscope]

1. Prepare the sample on the slide (you can section a portion of the culture with the scalpel or inoculate it).

2. Place it on the microscope stage.
3. Select your lens.
4. Bend in to take a look.
5. Adjust the focus with the side gear.
6. Be patient. These little critters might be stressed out at first.

The time has come to see you. The excitement is palpable given the haste of preparing the slides. I get in line. Ra places something on the stage, whatever it is that lives in the roots of a plant. Ce shows us how to focus. I bend down. I look, yearning to see. I turn the gear to focus, looking to see; we move between different planes. You are also on different planes. We are seeking to view the creatures we share a body with. Bacteria, fungi and so on. I catch myself, we catch each other, clambering to see.... The master's tools[98] are seductive. They do magical things[99]. Time becomes viscous and slow and our atten-

---

98. Her famous essay under the same name challenged racism in academic feminism in the 1980s, and urged feminists to abandon fields of knowledge that divide and conquer, as it demanded that the differences between women be centred as a source of knowledge and strength. May the echo of her voice remind us of the divisions that continue to exist and be re-produced by the knowledge apparatuses of petro-racial and patriarchal modernity. Lorde, Audre. 1984. "The Master's Tools Will Never Dismantle the Master's House." In Sister Outsider: Essays and Speeches, 110-14. Berkeley, CA: Crossing Press.

99. Magic, as an act of illusionism that offers what is observed as a fixed material reality, standing still in time, obscuring the relationship between

tion is trapped by the irresistible pull of the visuals, and the excitement to meet you. I look without knowing at what. Wanting to see you. I'm scanning for movement. What shape are you? How do you move? Are you found in a group? Or alone? We seek to know so we can see. *Is that one? Or how many of you are stuck together?* We see. Without knowing. *We have to give them time, let them chill out.* We change slides, a bit of your scalp and some of your vagina. The microscope and the giant image projected on the wall take me back to drive-in movies and natural science classes. *Can I make a video of your armpit?* There are two little wheels that move from side to side and another one that zooms in and out. I navigate switching between different planes. If I go a hair too far, everything gets blurred and I can't see anything... *Look, there's a big slow one.* When we catch some, we miss others. I remember that any act of observation makes a "cut" between what is included and what is excluded from the phenomenon being observed[100]. What are you looking at? *I've got a motorway in my pussy! It's like watching* TV, *but better.* We see through the lens of what we know. *A bird!*

Science isn't naïve, nor is it impartial. One of the origins of the microscope is the magnifying lens (tele-

observational practices and the worlds they create. Barad, Karen. 2007. Meeting the Universe Halfway: Quantum Physics and the Entanglement of Matter and Meaning. Second Printing edition. Durham: Duke University Press Books.

100. As Karen Barad proposes in her work on Agential Realism (Idem).

scope) that Galileo developed and offered to the Venetian Republic as a tool for military surveillance. The same one with which he validated Copernicus' heliocentric model that cost him being condemned by the Inquisition. Economic interests and epistemological disputes have certainly converged in the design and construction of this observation apparatus. Imbricated in the technology of looking through the microscope are the clinical testing of pharmaceuticals, as well as the study and development of biological weapons. What we observe is charged and composed by stories that produce reality. It matters what practices are practised.

[Holobiont yourself]

Choose a spot in the room, sit and make yourself comfortable.

Close your eyes.

Notice how the surface feels where you sit, where your feet rest. Release accumulated heaviness and tension. Relax your jaw, soften your eyes and let go of your mind. Allow gravity and the movement of your breath to cradle and support you. In this swaying, feel how, little by little, the ground becomes liquid, the edges of your organs dissolve and you assume the dimensions of a microscopic creature.

Imagine floating or being immersed in a juicy broth that envelops you and holds you at the same time. A PDA (Potato, Dextrose Agar[101]) medium that provides you with sugars, the energy necessary for your growth. Feel the density of the medium activating the different parts of you. You may become porous, glow or develop sucking trumpets. How do your organic and chemical components react in this environment? Let the medium nourish and mould you.

Other creatures share space with you. Fungi, yeasts, bacteria, protists (who knows[102]). Feel their fluctuations rippling through the gelatinous compound you inhabit. A flickering display that impacts your unicellular body, leaving you with the imprint of suggestive frequencies. Vibration - as an initial phylogenetic movement - is the degree of attraction or repulsion that underlies all movement, perception, intuition, organisation and relationship[103]. What oscillation, shake, or tremor moves you? You may be swept up in a current, turned on your axis by

101. https://en.wikipedia.org/wiki/Potato_dextrose_agar

102. "I kept thinking about protists, because they are not always single-celled. Protists also can be eukaryotic cells, like animals, plants and fungi. Even though there are millions of them, it's like a tailor's bag into which they throw everything that's still unclassifiable. That's what makes them so fascinating," said Ce, in response to an initial draft of this text.

103. Bainbridge Cohen, Bonnie. 2012. *Sensing, Feeling, and Action. The Experiential Anatomy of Body-Mind Centering*. 3rd edition. Toronto: Con-

a centripetal force, or propelled towards other bodies by an unstoppable attraction. Let the medium guide you.

Sense your molecular curiosity and unavoidable attraction to others. Who do you interact with? Who do you play with? Who do you avoid? What exchanges do you have with other bugs? How do you reproduce? What ripples of attraction and repulsion are you made up of? Perhaps an insatiable hunger, or an irresistible urge to envelop yourself is what mobilises your vital drive. You may interpenetrate with others, circulate around and through others, eat yourself, or be eaten. You may digest, you may assimilate, you may arrange yourself in assemblages, dynamic entanglements and contingencies[104]. Attune yourself to the possibilities created through intimacy with strangers. In this amalgam of co-creating bugs, you become part of a more complex relational being, configuring a holobiont. **Allow these improvised relationships to shape you.**

...pause

tact Editions. https://bonniebainbridgecohen.com/products/sensing-feeling-and-action.

104. Turning to Haraway's words of guided meditation. Haraway, Donna. 2016. Staying with the Trouble: Making Kin in the Chthulucene. Durham: Duke University Press.

Did you know that Darwin played at being a wasp[105] (an animal one), experimenting with his own body and sensing the erotic relationship between orchids and wasps[106]? Although we forget sometimes, the experimental method unites art and science: the container in which to test *what if*? What if we activate our imagination with somatic exercises and movement practices? How else can we access the metaphors of science? What other relationships can we configure when we activate somatic, intuitive, experimental apparatuses of observation? This Kriya, this guided meditation, kinesthetic imagination[107]/ felt

105. Read more in Hustak, Carla, and Natasha Myers. 2020. *Involutionary Momentum: Affective Ecologies and the Science of Plant/Insect Encounters*. Fold. https://medium.com/@fold/impulso-involuciona-rio-ee723ee27e9e.

106. "I was amazed by this talk we had while I was preparing the workshop and you were reading our book on the sofa. And you were saying all the time that you had the feeling that you didn't understand any of the book when you read it in English, even though you speak and write perfect English. It freaks me out in the sense that I think that these texts that we have commissioned from different people about the workshops that are taking place in Pluriversidad Nómada have something to do with that too: the texts are not a perfect chronicle of the workshop but rather they are provocations, because a chronicle, too, is always bastardised. The reading of a translated text or one that translates an action into text is inextricably linked to the bastardised. Translation from one format to another is also bastardised. It seems inevitable that in the reproducibility of an artefact, things are lost in the middle, even if new things also appear" said Ce, in response to the initial draft of this text.

107. The inspiration for designing this meditation was found in Natasha Myers' work. Myers, Natasha. 2014. A Kriya for Cultivating Your Inner

experiment is a bastardised practice in cuiring, making strange - modern taxonomic habits. A warm-up for new ways of knowing and imagining possible bugs. A training to sensitise ourselves to the relationships that compose us. A somato-kinesic activation to imagine cuir taxonomies. The preamble to a 3D taxonomy of microbial life in which X, X, X, X, X are connected. X eats Y and forms larger conglomerates, until other kingdoms develop.

[create a cuir atlas]

1. Draw and name your microscopic self.
2. Fill out a data sheet.
3. Distribute the sheets throughout the space.
4. Read them out loud.
5. Create links with coloured threads.

Atlases, offered as objects of "natural truth", veil the taxonomic practice - they hide the scientific/classificatory method which constitutes them, and offer the world as mere fixed representations, without life, histories or tensions. Although the antecedents of Western taxonomic classifications are attributed to Greek philosophers and physicians, modern taxonomic models superseded them,

Plant. UK: Centre for Imaginative Ethnography, Imagining Series Symposium. https://www.academia.edu/6467794/A_Kriya_for_Cultivating_Your_Inner_Plant.

not least thanks to the development of optical lenses that allowed the study of details of individual species. The emphasis shifted from medical to taxonomic aspects via the biologisation of medicine and the politicisation of the biological[108].

Modern taxonomic practice tries to find similarities, to create categories, consensus and worlds of individual beings with impermeable borders - *the plant and animal worlds cannot merge*. One fiction, another, of modern science. And an object of colonial knowledge that is far from being innocent.

> REMEMBER: *taxonomic classifications of human animals - the creation of racial differences - have served to justify mass plunder, kidnapping and genocide, and continue to sustain unequal distributive systems of risks and resources for life.*

Instead of a biocentric system of knowledge that assumes that we are wholly, completely and purely biological beings, bound to evolution and its teleological tem-

---

108. Specifically, I refer to the contamination between fields of knowledge, due to the theories of the physician and biologist Bichat on life, in which he proposed a division between vegetative life and active/rational life, which was then transferred to philosophy, politics and anthropology. This division would be used in anthropology at the time (the 19th century) to hierarchise human races. This current is explained in detail in the book: Martinez-Garcia, Miguel. 2021. *Bios, Literatura, Enfermedad, Formas de Vida*. Universitat de Valencia.

poralities, Katherine McKittrik proposes that we are physiological story-makers. Bio and myth. Creators of made-up evolutionary stories about our biological existences.[109] Can we imagine our past-present-future beyond colonial (biocentric) logic?

We spent some time writing and drawing; animating microscopic beings and naming them: *Hugh, Ater, Eman Oge Estractorus, Molinata Spiralis, Protista, exhuberantephylococa, Acufemus vibratoris, Oceanica -Fluorescence- 23, Espelmatron, luciferus magnus...* We filled in their data sheet: place of collection, mode of collection and description. We spread our "bugs" on the studio floor. We read aloud where you are found, how to collect you, what you do, what you like and what moves you. How you reproduce... and we begin making connections: these three share a sonic tendency, that one and this one vibrate at the same frequency. Maybe that one eats this one. I'm sure we're missing a lot.

In one hour we have our taxonomic composition: blue-pink-yellow tinted petri dishes with armpit, tear duct, mouth cultures, etc... interspersed with technical sheets and coloured threads. Like a set of string figures[110], which

109. McKittrick, Katherine. 2020. Dear Science and Other Stories. Durham: Duke University Press.

110. It reminds me of the string game that Donna Haraway uses as a metaphor in her text: Haraway, Donna Jeanne. "A Game of Cat's Cradle: Science

become a 3D taxonomic installation, bright woollen yarns tracing cuir classifications of microbiological worlds on different planes of reality. Protists hang from the ceiling, linked in a mystical category to X and Z. Other connections are indicated by their light and sound abilities, or because X eats O.

The installation is not a snapshot of something that exists "out there", or something frozen in time, but is rather the condensation of multiple material practices engaged in creating worlds. The set of practices entangled in the

IMAGES FROM THE WORKSHOP CUIR ATLAS / *SF:TRANS*PLANT* LED
BY CE QUIMERA. PHOTO: CARO NOVELLA.

Studies, Feminist Theory, Cultural Studies." Configurations 2, no. 1 (1994): 59-71. doi:10.1353/con.1994.0009.

sculpture-installation are: microbiology; open source activism; post-porn; optics; health activism; popular and feminist science; oracular, phylogenetic, and meditative practices; sheep breeding; yarn spinning; paper production; experimental dance; microscopy....

And it's "not only " a workshop

The emerging bio-mythological installation-sculpture encapsulates practices, and activates discursive currents at the crossroads. Art/science, expert/non-expert, bio/myth, human/nature, postporn/bioart. The knowledge that is generated is "strange" (cuir/queer) - it is outside the norms of science. That's the thing about art: it can (be) transcend(ed). Another friend comes to mind, Marisol de la Cadena, and I think with her and how she articulates the formula "not only", to point out this space of excess in the ethnographic translation between worlds. When entities are (and they aren't only one thing), but rather also what they could be - that piece we can't know[111]. It makes me think of this workshop, a singular exercise, which contains multiple practices, histories and relationships all at once.

111. de la CADENA, Marisol. 2014. "Runa, Human but *not only*" HAU: Journal of Ethnographic Theory. https://doi.org/10.14318/hau4.2.013.

A rebellious exercise,
to undiscipline ourselvesand merge knowledge.
A laboratory of bastard science.
Of cognitiverebellion.
Of armpit isotypes and cunt hairs
on paper towels, to look at.
A disruptor of the evolutionary trend.
A cuir atlas.
A restorative exercise in extracted knowledge.
An essay on bio-transformative justice, perhaps.
And not only these things.

Also present in this formula is the reality that translation can't capture everything, nor know everything, as Ce says, that translation is bastardised, that the artefact loses its ability to reproduce - in the limits of translation and in accepting that we can't know where a workshop begins/ends, and that "a" workshop is *not only* a workshop - that this device (text + workshop), playing with the materiality of science reminds us that it matters what practices enact which practices and that, at the crossroads, we're wagering on which worlds are made possible.

CA2 = RADIATING WHAT SPEECH DOESN'T CAPTURE

Tatiana Avendaño and Anaís Córdova-Páez

5, 6 and 7 July 2023, 4—8pm
Tabakalera – Donostia – Europe

TURNING OURSELVES INTO CLOUDS WITH A QUARTZ

Tatiana Avendaño

When Pluriversidad Nómada decided to invite Anaís Córdova-Páez and myself to participate in their 2023 programme, with the workshop "Ca2 =radiating what speech doesn't capture", we wanted to invoke the conductive powers of the soft metal that is Calcium (Ca) - the main element in our bones, which makes the skeleton our most powerful antenna - to amplify the research of Cuerpx Antenx and perhaps radiate through experimental cinema what speech doesn't capture, which may be something similar to what the internet can't transfer or store on its own. In the workshop we explore the possibilities of data transmission, waves, frequencies and sensations of different materials, as an invitation to continue probing the unlimited and galactic powers of the Cuerpx itself.

The non-magic of interconnectedness, instantaneity and borderless simultaneity - depending on who and where - of the internet is real thanks to an infrastructure, which is the interweaving of a physical layer[112] and another that is logical[113] , which has as its epicentre the "western" north, and which has been built upon (and with) the old structure of colonial domination and oppression. This blissful immateriality, which has given so much to write and think about in the cloisters of that same north, has brought vaporous ideas that paved the way for an even bigger distance between one another, as well as between us and everything in our surroundings (including technology).

This is how technology has been instrumental in deepening the "sensitivity gap", which is the separation between us and life. If we think that everything that technology does is something that the elements already do in their different states in this sphere called Earth, and that we are made of the same elements, perhaps we can develop practices that allow us to activate our body's abilities for transmission. Trying to bridge this gap, Ca2 proposed several exercises that had in common activating our bodies' power to transmit (the physical layer), and exploring alliances with new materials trying to activate other powers of our logical layer.

112. Copper cables, fibre optics, antennas, servers, routers and modems.

113. Software, protocols, policies and agreements, standards and configurations.

Quartz has been a strategic element in the development of technology, not only for its piezoelectric abilities, but also for its great capacity to store information and generate stable and constant frequencies. At Ca2 we work with herkimer diamonds, a small quartz with no "root", and therefore in its formation process it pulled a large amount of information from the galaxy, making it a strategic ally in the development of telepathy.

Ca2 was a space to invite other bodies to be part of this experimentation, to turn ourselves into clouds with a quartz, to question the immateriality of the internet, and to make use of the resources of experimental cinema to radiate what speech doesn't capture. This text doesn't reflect everything that could begin to be mineralised in those three days of the workshop.

TELEPATHIC EXPERIENCES OR CONVERSATIONS WITH OTHER SPECIES

Anaís Córdova-Páez

The absence/presence of light was detected by our ancestors and a gradual adaptation to the environment, conditions and pressures of the ecosystem resulted in the formation of the ocelli, a kind of primitive eye comprising several photosensitive cells that perceive light, but not images. At some point this system reformulated into that of the complex eye, leaving an evolutionary memory of light and its presence in our ganglia. The window of the visual has its functioning underpinned in the sensory system of our bodies. Visioning, therefore, does not happen only through the eyes. It is the body that understands and sees.

In a world where technocapitalism fills us with "technological solutions" to keep its model afloat, remembering the senses, evolutionary and personal processes, critiquing them, coming together to experiment and explore other ways of communicating, are palpable ways to address this crisis. As we allow ourselves to feel, we expand the possibility to experiment and question.

Ca2 = radiating what speech doesn't capture was a call to live an experience designed to activate the whole, a loving place where using our hands evoked another language: the language of dreams. It placed value on our relationships with non-human beings, all of which was intended to radiate ideas, frequencies, energy that crosses from one body to another. To radiate as a whole is a poetic, anti-systemic act. It opens the possibility of other forms of communication, of transforming science into experiment, and experiment into cinema.

Drawing from collage techniques based on experimental film allows us to speak from other feelings with ourselves, creating a space to experiment without seeing, to listen to the 16mm projector, and to place our attention on sensations. The joint creation of moving image also emphasised collective filmmaking as a new language that moves between dreams and telepathy.

In addition to engaging others, this collective proposal was a coming together of two artistic practices that have been accompanying each other in relationship. We are constantly telepathically communicating with Tatiana (or is it the other way around?), in keeping with the need to create other forms of human and non-human families.

"Ca2 = radiating what speech doesn't capture" took some western scientific knowledge and mixed it with the body, dreams and experimentation, making knowledge more our own and less that of others.

FREQUENCY, APERTURE, TREMOR
[some notes to record that which radiates]

danele sarriugarte mochales

note

this text is a loose record of the workshop "Ca2= irradiar aquello que el habla no atrapa" ("Ca2=radiating what speech doesn't capture"), organised by pluriversidad nómada and facilitated by tatiana avendaño and anaís córdova-páez on 5, 6 and 7 july 2023 at the tabakalera centre in donostia[114].

114. i want to thank ce quimera and lucía egaña for their work and for the invitation to write, tatiana and anaís for their time, attention, knowledge and practices, itziar imaz and oihane espúñez for the space and faciliation, and the comrades who participated, for sharing and connecting. thank you all for your trust and your warmth.

starting

to begin, we take part in an activation exercise by lightly tapping ourselves with our fists from our ankles to our head. we breathe. some of us close our eyes. there are those who sigh and those who yawn. we try to tune into a frequency, a particular frequency. in some spots the tapping of fists serves as a greeting, a kind of recognition, especially in the case of my legs that anchor and sustain me. i feel life tingling in the soles of my feet. in other places the tapping makes me tender, soft places like the belly, the lower back or the breasts. tapping my shoulders i feel the load i'm carrying, and i have to stay there for a long while until i stop wincing and my breath finally expands. upon reaching my face and my hair, my fists become caressing fingers. then we sit.

writing

for me writing is also about connecting with a certain kind of frequency, a certain rhythm, that *wave in the mind*: once you reach that rhythm *it's impossible to get the words wrong*, once *the wave breaks and settles*[115] the words start to fit. words that can be chewed[116], *words endowed*

---

115. following virginia woolf's expression coming to me through ursula k. le guin. *the wave in the mind: talks and essays on the writer, the reader, and the imagination*, shambala publications, boston, 2004.

116. ixiar rozas, *sonar la voz. 9 ensayos y 9 partituras* consonni, bilbao, 2022.

with the power to crawl along the ground[117]. upon writing i invoke and surround myself with others, and today before lying down with a laptop on my thighs i read the last pages of a book that anaís recommended to me, that was physically present in the z-room where we did the workshop, the z-room where we indulged in an activation exercise by lightly tapping ourselves with our fists from our ankles to our heads before sitting down.

the book was on a table, one full of coloured markers. the book is called *imaginación material (material imagination)* by andrea soto calderón and today, before i begin writing this, i underline the following: *thought is possible thanks to the fingertips, where the hand no longer moves from one point to another, but the insistent gesture of our modes of production of images and thought, even textual thought, passes through the hand's grasp,* and also this: *the point is that we type blindly, we initiate processes of which, in most cases, we are completely unaware of their workings,* and finally this: *the concept of speculative groping refers to the way in which we approach something carefully, without placing expectations and meanings that have been fixed beforehand.*[118]

117. zafra, remedios. *ojos y capital*, consonni, bilbao, 2015, p. 15.

118. andrea soto calderón, *imaginación material*. ediciones metales pesados, santiago de chile, 2022, p. 137.

dreaming

sitting down, we talk about our dreams, our dreams in the literal sense, not the figurative: recurring dreams, recent dreams, dreams we always have. i rarely remember what i dream, i know that i often settle scores and in the end that is what i say, that i recently dreamt of a conversation with someone, someone who in waking life had taken my hand one night and with whom i had formed for some time a powerful, but finite, orbit of friendship.

of that dream, more than words, i remembered the feeling: an embrace, a kind of closure.

some people say that they have a whole parallel life in their dreams, a dream identity of their own with places they know from their sleep and scenes that take place outside the other life, the waking life - think of selver and the village of athshe, protagonists of the novel *the name of the world is forest* by ursula k. le guin[119], for whom dreaming is a method and a source of knowledge. there are those who prefer not to share because lately they only have nightmares. it is suggested to them that when waking from a bad dream, to turn their pillow over.

tatiana tells us that for a long time she wrote them down - i'm thinking of itziar okariz's book of dreams[120] - and that she did so as soon as she woke up, still in an

119. i discovered this novel thanks to the basque translation by amaia apalauza: ursula k. le guin, oihan hitzean mundua, igela argitaletxea, iruñea, 2021.

120. itziar okariz, *sueños*, caniche editorial, bilbao, 2022.

inbetween state, lying in bed, before what had been so vivid became undone. *imagination* i think, [like dreams?] is seldom considered a sort of agency. it is at best *understood as that which makes us do, but not a specific way of doing. nevertheless, imagination configures ways of doing, it is always performative in the sense that it articulates ways of tracing, desiring, affecting and inhabiting reality. it is an inventive doing*[121], and i think of you, of course. you, the one who dreamed so hard and remembered so much, the one whose imagination was always forging something.

taking charge

we are electromagnetic fields after all, and falling in love is also a certain kind of connection, a certain energy, a certain tremor. it's not that i need more reason to think about you but that day in particular, the day i offered myself to an activation exercise by tapping myself with my fists from my ankles to my head before sitting with others in a circle in tabakalera's z-room to share our dreams, dreams in the literal sense, not in the figurative, recent dreams, recurring dreams, the same dreams we always have, in my case sliding the beads of an abacus upon finite orbits of friendship, configuring a balance sheet, and that day which is 5 july 2023, ce mentions you because she knows you and told you about the workshop being held, in the same way last week anaís mentioned you because

121. *Ibid*, p. 55.

she knows you and had told you about the talk by lucrecia masson we were heading to. lucrecia masson, whose
ruminative writings also accompany me while i write this
text, in an *attempt* [among many other things] *to look
around and not forward*[122].

so, in the space of a week, the week between june and
july, twice i come to believe that you will be there, that
we will see each other, but in the end we don't. then, a
few days later, we meet, a month after taking charge and
distancing ourselves. when you arrive at the café nervión
i'm already there. you look at me from the door and smile
your smile at me. i come closer, we embrace. our frequency
radiates differently. there is something else. closing and
opening. a modulation. energy that doesn't disappear but
rather transforms itself.

compass

in the workshop i do things i haven't done since i was
a child. magnetising, tracing, painting. experimenting,
testing. wondering about the basic functioning of simple
technologies that i use every day. within a compass there is
room for the colonial order of the world. a compass works
by means of geomagnetism. i would have said before that
a compass points north by means of geomagnetism, but
the truth is what the compass is showing is a south-north

---

122. lucrecia masson, *escrituras rumiantes. cuerpo, exceso, animalidad*, pajarera libertaria, bogotá, 2022.

axis, both directions. to privilege one of them, to paint one pole red and eliminate the other is a decision, a concrete and violent configuration of the world.

we make our compass the following way: we rub a needle against a magnet for a while, then we place it along the centre of a round cork, so that it runs from side to side. ideally we should be able to pierce the centre from one end, pushing down and sideways into the cork until the other tip of the needle pokes up and out on the opposite side, to keep it fastened. i try, but in the end i have to place the needle on top, securing it with tape. we put our compasses in a tupper full of water to float. trembling, expectation, some interference due to the plastic of the container and the amount of compasses it contains. but after a while the waves settle and our compasses mark the south axis - pulling a little to the west - and the north axis - pulling a little to the east.

one of the problems is *the belief that has been formed through the arduous work of erasure by dominant cultures, that there are no other valid ways of doing, other modes of critical existence and other ways of living. they exist, but they have been stifled almost to the point of extinction*[123]. in the case of the cardinal points, there are four of them, and each one has its own frequency - its function: in the east is born the flame that kindles a desire; to the south

123. andrea soto calderón, *op. cit.*, p. 45.

it grows, develops; to the west comes the time to end it; to the north souls rest after death.

tabakalera

the building we're in, a huge building, was, as its name suggests, a tobacco factory and is now a contemporary art centre in a central enclave for the process of touristi-fication overtaking the city. tabakalera's mediation area, which houses this workshop, is one of the initiatives i know best, because friends have been and are part of it, and because of the way in which they understand medi-ation - based on feminisms and intersections, in contact with the community, with the neighbourhood, with the plural realities and the real public that day by day creates the building, always upholding the memory of those women who entered and left this concrete giant to the wails of factory sirens, who in the meantime worked, laughed, fought and wove collectivity -, from that per-spective i have learnt a lot and we have learnt a lot. we shall see if it continues.

one of the recent projects being developed at tab-akalera, and which i'm gradually getting to know, above all through those who have taken part in it - because this concrete block, apart from being large, can be hermetic - is the film school. when they started it up i had already been living in the neighbourhood, the egia neighbour-hood, for a few years, and i began to note the presence of the school when i realised that i regularly saw a group of unknown people, more or less always the same group, in the bar downstairs, the riojanos' bar. i remember i noticed a person who wore glasses with mid-length hair, almost always dressed in black clothes, and although she looked very serious, as she talked, she gesticulated as if a fire were burning inside. i kept looking at her from afar for a while and then i couldn't, she left. the group of strangers i found regularly around eight o'clock in the evening in the bar remained, but now it was made up of others. i suppose she graduated. fortunately there are those who stay after they've finished the programme. fortunately there are those i've got to know more than by sight, thanks to little cracks opened up by mutual friends in the wall that basque sociability sometimes becomes.

ritual

we paint directly on a reel of 16 mm film. everyone gets a strip of film that's a bit too long and they work on it: some people make stripes and marks on it with a felt-tip pen, some people make holes in it, some people stick hair on it and some people paint it with nail polish. i choose the latter because i like the idea, and they tell me it dries quickly, which doesn't hurt. we also speed up the drying sometimes with a hairdryer. we join our strips together until they form a single film, our film. we do this with tape and a manual machine, i'm shown what to do and i stick my little strip to the other colleagues' on each side. they set up the projector on the not very high platform on one

side of the room, winding the film on a reel. laura, a col-
league from the workshop, opens the guts of the projector
and inserts the roll so that we can see the film, our film.
we walk around her and look at her fingers as she does
this; because of the lighting arrangement in the room -
only the 16 mm machine itself is lit, with the screens of
our mobiles hovering around, the thick curtains drawn
- the two reels cast shadows high on the wall with our
heads surrounding them.

it seems like a ritual, for me it is.

we projected the film, it's beautiful. a minute and a half
of light and moving colours.

we watch it several times, noticing one detail or another,
applauding from the inside each time. to me, honestly,
it seems unreal and magical, but i've seen how it's made,
step by step. we've made it together.

dancing
the workshop also extends beyond our session. when
it's over we eat and drink, we chat. some of us go to an
electronica party where a friend plays. dancing is one of
the practices in which i feel i radiate the most. dancing
vibrates and connects me with sound frequencies, waves
in movement, magnetism pulls me towards the floor
and towards other bodies. dancing is how we started to

become friends with anaís, on this same dance floor where we are today after the workshop. dancing is what the little book i recommended to her the first time we both went to a bookshop was about. *just like sex, dancing is a practice of low intensity alterity. we don't always do it in the same way, we are not always the same when we do it. [...] sex is never just sex. dancing is never just dancing either*[124].

it's the same book i'd recommended to you some time ago, because it was also through dancing that you and i connected. actually i lent it to you at first, but you loved it so much you told me you wanted your own copy to underline everything everything everything. *dancing is a relationship between bodies mediated by music as a surface of contact. dancing is a form of communication through a borrowed language. it is also a technology of emotional synchronisation thanks to the material and gestural syn-chronisation of bodies. by picking up and assimilating each other's movements, we communicate through each other's language. otherness becomes plural. we are many at once, we are a multitude in a single body. to be is to become. to be implies contagion and not essence. gestures do not belong to us: it is us who belong to them, it is they who activate the dancing community*[125].

124. sonia fernández pan, *edit*, caniche editorial, bilbao, 2022, pp. 34-35.
125. *Ibid*, p. 35.

coda

today the mood of the room is a bit off, i don't feel fully connected, vibrating only half-heartedly or in brief moments. it's a shared feeling, and little by little we start leaving. later that night, sleeping in bed, i review my balance sheet: i dream of us dancing until dawn. we are the dance, the frequency, we are antennae-bodies. we are the waves of sound, the light in movement, the embraces, the sweat.

it's a relative closure: we continue to radiate.

LISTENING TO A STONE

Tau Luna Acosta

2 and 3 September 2023, 11am—5pm
Wetlab, Hangar – Barcelona – Europe

If we pay attention we can hear the Earth creaking as it turns on its own axis. It is a very slow movement, barely perceptible to humans for their impatience, but real to all the beings that inhabit it and make it what it is.

Juan Rulfo

To undertake this process of openness and shared experience, my departing point was attention as a muscle to be exercised, in order to be able to perceive invisible fields of life-sustaining forces.

Through attention and the experience of existence, humans are part of the permanent production of worlds; cosmopolitics, of everything that is part of living together on Earth. "Life is a force itself" proposes *Krenak*, it is not something merely there, as something to be used or occupy space; it *exerts itself* as a continuous force between bodies, matter, worlds and existence.

I started with this question because of my own relationship with $Fe2+Fe3+2O4$ (magnetite), a mineral with which I have been working since 2020, and has accompanied me on my journey as a migrant in Spain. Due to its atomic composition, it has an electric field that makes it a natural magnet, and given magnetite is found in huge quantities in the innermost layer of the Earth, this is the reason why it becomes a giant magnet. Throughout my alliance with the stone I've discovered that in addition to being part of the Earth's core, and appearing on its surface as volcanic rock and crystals, it's also found in the bodies of migratory species of animals and bacteria, giving them the perceptive field of magnetoception, which is the ability of these bodies to sense geomagnetic fields, and thus locate themselves in order to know where to go when beginning their own migratory journeys, and how to return to their starting point.

The workshop took place over two days, as two 6-hour intensive sessions, with a break for lunch as a group, so I divided each day into two blocks; one before and one after lunch. Each participant was asked before the meeting to bring their own mineral, which would be their working tool and path opener during the workshop.

The four blocks consisted of a series of collective rhythmic practices, deep listening, collective reading, writing and collaborative embroidery based on mineral cartographies.

Each block of exercises began with the company of a plant that acted as a starter to get us ready for the activities.

Thinking from and with magnetite allows me to think about the sun, as a force that creates life while at the same time has an enormous power to create death. And to ask myself questions about the nature of human time in relation to that of mineral time, and how this discrepancy in scales affects the blindness of the colonial order to the life of mineral bodies.

During the workshop we mapped our mineral relationships and the - real or imagined - geopolitical and
migratory histories of each mineral and stone invited
into our hands: drilling, exploitation, excavation,
exploration, extraction. Crushing, grinding, leaching,
exporting, disease, death, water, bone, medicine, cancer,
pharmacy, ritual, time, lead, necropolitics, repression,
healing, autonomy.

Like any body, a stone is an archive, which can be
asked about the history of all life on earth. From these
questions we can glimpse our possibilities of alliance and
commitment to care, and mineral reciprocity.

TO WEAVE A REFLECTIVE STORYLINE: LISTENING TO A STONE

Thais de Menezes

This text rehearses grappling with a movement, a series of questions on Tau's workshop entitled *Listening to a Stone*. I start off with reflections that were initiated during the discussion that took place in the workshop, without pretending that they can be answered and/or closed at the end of the text, or even summarise the workshop. My approach is quite the opposite. What's in dialogue are traces of journeys lived during the process, and incorporated into black skin that's stitched, migrant, and soaked with the water, salt and sun of the South Atlantic. And as such, the different subjectivities that make up the historical-social crystallisations of a black sapatão[126] migrant Latina who insists, insists and insists on questioning.

listen > hear > listen > listen > listen

The opening of the experience led by Tau is a discussion on the different interpretative forms between hearing and listening, an important agreement for the collective encounter proposed by the artist. In this context, drawing attention to the title of the workshop, which carries within itself the desire to listen, I pose the following question:

1. How to create a body, a life experience committed to the different possibilities of listening to something beyond oneself?

Although unanswered - which for me is of deep interest - I review a few salient points of the act of listening evoked here: approach, body and openness of the senses. There is a fundamental element in the title of the workshop that corresponds to all poetic and investigative endeavours: the stone. In this case, listening is guided by a human body and directed towards a mineral. Here the spotlight shines on the interspecies relationship.

126. sapatão: tortillera, bollera, tortillera, camiona, maricona, arepera, all expressions to name lesbians in Spanish in Abya Yala.

< approach > body > opening of the senses >

The ideas of approximation embedded in the human experience of listening as discussed by the artist, cause us to look at the interaction we commonly have with a mineral.

2. Is it possible to have an approach in which the whole human body strives to allow for different possibilities of receiving new ideas on the mineral presented, without the historical relational experience of extraction guiding that encounter?

Tau includes magnetite as a mineral of interest in their work, however, the discussion expands, inviting those present to reflect on their own relationships with various rocks. And each participant produced an individual map reflecting on the question:

3. "How did the mineral you brought today come to you?" -Tau.

Reflection on this reveals the violent power of mineral extraction, as well as questions of migration, violence and nature. Bodies forced to migrate because existence in a certain place is no longer possible due to voracious extermination policies, is also a reality shared by members of the workshop.

Chip up. Cut. Break. Scramble. Abandon. Exhaust.
Transfigure.

The verbs used above to reflect on Tau's question, pierce human and more-than-human bodies with the same level of power and violence, as well as the territories that compose them.

I, Thais de Menezes, black everywhere I have been. A woman in the widest possible sense of the word. Sapatão in the experience of a sexuality that breaks with colonial desire. Latin immigrant living in Barcelona. I migrated in 2018 with my dearest companion and our cats to Europe. I understood that my life was at stake given the rise of Bolsonaro's presidency, and all the deadly force his administration represented. Of course, it was nothing new to have my life at risk being who I am, but in this case it would be hard to live. So there is also an "extraction" of lives that are sometimes forced to migrate, even to go into exile, because it becomes impossible to experience their territory, sexuality, political convictions, raciality or beliefs with dignity and "safety".

Among some animals, other than humans, a behavioural modification in their migratory movements is also perceived, due to the climatic impact of human actions. An example of this phenomenon is the case of the Sabiá bird, very present in the territories where I live in southeastern Brazil. The three subspecies of this bird have seen their breeding territory systematically reduced, a situation that affects their survival.

The decrease and/or loss of territory is a shared experience, given that the cis-hetero-white capitalist colonialist system is itself a systemic violence that permeates everything with its overwhelming power of death and destruction.

mountain > sheets > souvenirs > abandonment

Philosopher, environmentalist and poet Ailton Krenak (2020) reflects on consumption through the devastation of mountains, and draws attention to the process of transforming them into aspects other than their original state in order to be consumed by humans.

The ore is taken out of the mountains and turned into sheets (...) A mountain is turned into sheets of ore for the manufacture of cars and household appliances, frying pans, refrigerators, which never become a mountain again. It is one mountain less upon the organism of the Earth. Metals and all the other materials that are used do not come back. The concept of recycling is recycling for further consumption. It is not a return to nature. The oceans are depleted by everything we take from them, plus littering. There are pits in the ocean that have mountains of plastic in them. In other words, we are destroying natural mountains on the surface and creating artificial mountains in the ocean trench[127] .

127. KRENAK, Ailton. 2020. A vida é Selvagem. Cadernos SELVAGEM. Rio de Janeiro. Dantes Editora Biosfera.

I can relate Krenak's reflections on the transformation of (natural) mountains into (artificial) plastic mountains to some videos on mineral extraction presented by Tau. The images show trains, people and rural areas. Dark bodies with worn-out clothes and the landscape covered by a yellowish dust. There is a portrait of bodies and territories subjected to a state of deep exhaustion and death. It is a pile of people; a mountain of bodies exhausted by the extraction of minerals, with dust formed by particles of earth blowing in the wind from what was once a mountain.

4. How to listen to a mountain of exhausted (natural) bodies while transforming the (natural) mountain into sheets and souvenirs?

The questions posed can be situated on the border between epistemology (what and how one can know) and ontology (what one is), which in Tau's poetics are presented as the process of interspecies approaching each other to listen. My effort to ensure that there is no desire to exhaust, to end, to close questions, is a methodology for reflecting on/in this essay. Thus, I will carry on with my investigative exercise, and perhaps by the time you read this, many things will have already changed. This is only a speculative trace of a specific topic in the midst of the complexity of thought shared by the artist. However, such traces will allow me to return to the fissures that remain open to research, and not the perverse entrapment that is the great investigation *Listening to a stone*.

tracks < research > movements >
opening of the body

In order not to finish, but to continue with the imaginative effort that could draw other thinkers and different epistemologies closer to each other for reflective follow-up, I leave with a question by Gabriela that moved me the most during our collective experience:

5. What are the rocks that make up my body?

Which brings me to the next question:

6. Would the rocks that make up my body, together with the rocks that exist beyond me, propose other listening experiences in relationship to one another?

CONFABULATING
AND IMAGINING THE END
OF THIS WORLD
[Speculative writing workshop]

Lucía Egaña Rojas

9 and 10 September 2023, 11am—5pm
La Parcería – Madrid – Europe

This workshop was conceived as a space for temporal disorder. A space for time travel with the aim of piercing and neutralising the narratives around life that are framed within patriarchal, colonial and capitalist visions. We are surrounded by descriptions of the world from technosolutionary, extractivist and uncontrolled perspectives. These technologies are presented to us as tools that solve problems, while at the same time they puncture the planet, bodies and especially certain voices with their violence. That is why I was interested in experimenting with writing understood as an ancestral technology, a way of creating realities of any time, and a strategy for the exercise of narrative justice.

I am convinced that transfeminist and anti-racist perspectives and visions could turn some of these problems into other powers and circumstances. Capable of transmuting the weight of violence through narrative agency to create, at best, exercises in healing, re-appropriation, transformation and recognition of that which has been historically erased, to the point of having rendered its existence nearly impossible.

In the workshop we came together to speculate on the (im) possible in ways that challenge normative knowledge and the affirmative power of those who have always embodied the same, single, presumably universal subject. Our speculations on the future, present and past to come, sought to relate to each other so that through their union, congregation and repetition, we could close gaps, recompose scenes and create new places of possibility.

We met at La Parcería, a migrant and anti-racist space in the city of Madrid on the 9th and 10th of September 2023. During these two immersive days we spent most of the time writing, eating and sharing a creative and speculative space. I proposed a series of exercises, related to past and future memories of each participant. Exercises that questioned one's own subjectivity, territorial memories, the possibilities of ceasing to be human, the slogans of the minuscule, forming words between different bodies that have become letters, writing in uncomfortable positions, ceasing to be, being with others and creating spaces of communal affection for listening and one's own voice. I believe we enjoyed it quite a bit, and I treasure the hours together, their possibility of temporary extension, and of being an amulet of protection against the unimaginable.

BECOMING PLURAL[128]

María Bajo, Romina Casile, Ana CSC,
Elízabeth Manjarrés Ramos, Valeska Morales
Urbina, Iria Rodríguez, Roberta Stubs, Nur
Tissera, Sophia Wong.

128. Selection by Lucía Egaña from the texts that some workshop participants voluntarily shared to be published in this book.

To become a textile maker yourself, using your own hands, is to take the reins of what that covers as you go about exploring the ruins of the world. While before you could forget about the whole process behind each polo shirt, skirt or trousers, you now understand the genuine cost. With your own labour behind each garment, a much more balanced and non-hierarchical exchange occurs. You and your fellow workers can express individual creativity through what is implemented in each piece, imbuing the social fabric with inherent value.[...] This way, we can all stop running ourselves ragged, navigating a thousand activities and demands: that belonged to the capitalism we've defeated. We also organise ourselves to be able to produce our own fabric, even making extra for those who can't. Always reminding each other: never hesitate to ask for help, if you get tangled up with a stitch. You already have everything you need to get started, and there are thousands of techniques. That's the great thing about fabrics, of course they're a necessity, but they also allow us to explore each step of the creative process. May we continue weaving together knowledge, to protect ourselves and continue to heal this Earth.

& at the
supposed
end of
the world
I see them
petrified,
wanting to
be like us.

Recoiling from linear time
Turning back to the ancestral song
The call of emotion
To the beat of the drums

THE STONES BORE WITNESS TO THE CLAMOUR IN THE STREETS,
THE WORLD BURNING AROUND THEM,
NOTHING WOULD EVER BE THE SAME AGAIN.
A SOCIAL EARTHQUAKE,
THAT TRANSFORMED LIFE/DEATH/LIFE,
GROANS, LAMENTATIONS,
OF MUTILATED HUMANITY,
ANNIHILATED AND FRAGMENTED,
BLINDED EYES,
DEAF EARS,
BEFORE THE PLEAS OF PAIN.
DIS-HUMANITY
IT'S NOW TIME TO HEAR THEIR CRIES

These cries, PREGNANT WITH THE FUTURE
and their ancestral voices

THEY SET ME ON FIRE.

My words are never what they appear to be but something else.

When I say
"mountain",
I am speaking about
the vibratory power
of all the material
bodies of the world.
That something else
is felt on my skin.
That something else
I can talk about, but
I can't capture: an
energy pulsating.

I'm sewing seeds in the cracks in the ground, hiding the magma under the blanket of mantle. Irritants are the best. At first a couple of minutes will suffice, but as I get used to the pain I'll have to hold out for longer before I get to feel true pleasure. The crust beats on both sides, pumping the lava up the vent. First the fumarole turns purple, then the crater white. The time has come: flowers release one by one, savouring the catharsis. On this path to training torment, readings will later fulfil the same function as these initial fruits that were born.

My identity has never been characterised by humanity. For what is humanity if not a description of the neuro-logically normative?

My grandfather, in his nineties, with his wrinkled and almost inert body, will leave behind the legacy of his oppression after his death. My mother passes on to me the post-traumatic stress that I drag wherever I can, making me a monster in body and soul.

Waterfall without
gravity

Still wetness,
not rushing

Waterfall
without gravity
      They said I'm not on the right track
      In overwhelm
            I   j u s t   o v e r f l o w e d
            Still wetness,
            not rushing
                  They said I'm not on
                  the right track

Immersed in darkness

V.V.A.A.

most of the time, damp, wet, slippery,
I could be likened to a mollusc, an
invertebrate body, curved and changeable.
Unsettled and unsettling. I tend to be
a fertile territory where intensities of
elements coming from outside can be
explored, but also where the sounds of
words that emerge from the throat flow.

Sometimes I set out in search of others like me. First
I extend myself to the contact of another's lips that
in their openness make the encounter possible. Once
in contact, one with the other, we move, wetter than
before, exchanging fluids and flavours.

Sometimes I work better with some than
with others. It's a question of rhythms, of
timing, of surrender. When I finish, as
an exercise of slow retreat, I return to my
concavity, and the drool of another body

173

remains with me, for a while, on my surface.

Very early on I developed a fixation with water.
I would wet little pieces of paper
in the school sink.
I would wet the corners of some of the pages
of my
favourite books and dry them with my fingers
in a second.
I did this to remind my
future self
that my past self
had been
there.

RECOMMENDATIONS FOR
BEFORE WHAT'S AFTER

▷ Resist the imperative to constantly do.

▷ Watch the clouds drift by whenever they're there.

▷ Train your voice, to speak, to sing, to celebrate.

▷ Give love, lots of it.

▷ Don't do more than one thing at a time.

▷ Eat fruits and save seeds.

▷ Always carry a pencil and notebook.

▷ Avoid arrogant people and hierarchical spaces.

▷ Relax.

▷ Drink water and stay hydrated.

▷ Always have a tent ready.

▷ Celebrate loved ones.

▷ Learn to wrap a T-shirt around your head; treasure stomach protectors to protect your eyes.

▷ Think about what three things you would take to a desert island, what five things you would save from a fire. Collect them and put them in a backpack.

▷ Watch that Hollywood romcom you secretly want to, you'll never get to watch it again.

▷ Grab your friends by the hand and go join the hackers; go to the ritual site.

▷ Meditate and create your own mantras.

▷ Organise and distribute work at meal times.

▷ Eat something sweet to help calm your nerves and boost your energy.

▷ Say goodbye to those you think will disappear.

▷ Write a letter which will prevail, lest you too fade away.

▷ Look for another profession or livelihood, because the academy is probably going to disappear.

▷ Make a community to care for them in a sustainable way.

▷ At this point, groups of farmers and livestock keepers will be able to produce sustainable food.

▷ Make others aware of the singularity of their personality.

▷ Take care of your body.

▷ Cultivate your mind, nourish yourself with people and stories, weave together human webs in which to seek refuge when the known world collapses.

▷ Learn trades and old technologies.

▷ Seek forms of food sovereignty.

▷ Build new ways of communicating, generate circles of security.

▷ Learn to live less and less dependent on the god of capital.

▷ Go out and enjoy a starry sky in solitude, without the fear of being raped, murdered and buried.

▷ Do without clothes, unless it's winter.

▷ Collect male tears, in case there is a drought.

▷ Learn to really enjoy yourself, allow yourself to learn a musical instrument or use your own body to make melodies.

▷ Get rid of what you know to be a family, and allow yourself to create your own tribe.

▷ Honour your father and mother.

▷ Take a mirror and practise neutral acceptance.

▷ Have a pack of cards on hand for recreational/leisure time, and play a few games with your fellow revolutionaries.

▷ Feel free to invent a world in which you can fit your overflow.

▷ Pick your best pair of shoes and lace them up well, they will be very useful for jumping over cracks.

▷ Embrace your fellow survivors.

▷ Be prepared to leave taxonomic divisions behind in order to join your non-human comrades.

▷ Try to remember all the non-digital technologies you were taught for getting around in the new world.

▷ Train our bodies to walk long distances.

▷ **Don't lose your south[129].**

129. Don't lose your way. The colonist way of saying this is "don't lose your north", we prefer don't lose your south.

BIOGRAPHIES

Anaís Córdova-Páez

is dedicated to reflecting on how politics, ecology, gender and moving images dialogue with each other in the age of the internet. Her work centres care by challenging established processes of film production and exhibition. She experiments with film, and programmes EQUIS Festival de Cine Feminista (Ecuador) and UNSEEN (Croatia).

Caro Novella Centellas

Catalan, white, transfeminist crip artist-mediator-researcher working across research-creation, feminist science, and the experimental movement arts. In 2011, I created *oncogrrrls*, in 2018 started *co-sense lab*, and in 2021 got my PhD in Performance Studies from University of California, Davis. Currently, I teach, mentor, write and facilitate creative processes on arts and health. I aim to cultivate humility, play and move very slowly.

Ce Quimera

my research and practice is situated in the field of art and deals with questions surrounding identities and technosciences, while endeavouring to not lose sight of a firm commitment to collective knowledge. I approach anthropology, biology and interspecies relations in an undisciplined, transfeminist, cuir/queer and anticolonial way. I am part of Quimera Rosa, Pluriversidad Nómada, and curate/take care of projects at Hangar Wetlab. If you look for me by my ID number I would be Cecilia Puglia Gonzalez but I prefer to be called Ce Quimera.

danele sarriugarte mochales

writes and translates. she has published two novels and several short stories, and has translated works by audre lorde and eva illouz, among others,
into basque. a regular contributor to the press, for media such as argia and
pikara magazine, she participates in the transfeminist and queer movement
in donostia (euskal herria).

iki yos piña funes

Maroon-fugitive. caribeñx, writer, performer, illustrator. Their research
focuses on anti-colonial archives and sexual dissidence, black Caribbean
memories and ancestral spiritualities and times. She is part of the Colectivo
Ayllu, the Cooperativa Periferia Cimarrona, and the experimental group for
radical black thought "in the wake" at Espacio Afro in Madrid.

Kina Madno

is co-founder and member of Quimera Rosa - www.quimerarosa.net - a
laboratory for experimentation and research on identities, bodies and technosciences, created in Barcelona in 2008. She currently lives in Athens where
she participates in the project Amoqa: Queer arts and politics
- www.amoqa.net - and is working on writing a science fiction novel.

Lucía Egaña Rojas

I am dedicated to art, writing, research, pedagogy and practices of self-in-
stitutionalisation, situated between the kingdom of spain, and latin america,
Abya/Yala. I deal with feminisms and sexuality, methodologies, technology,
North-South power relations, colonial and migratory processes, extractivism
and error. I have been part of various collectives, and am currently
co-coordinating Pluriversidad Nómada.
http://luciaegana.net

Lucrecia Masson Córdoba

Always maintaining impurity as a principle, she is a writer, researcher and artist. Her main themes of enquiry are bodies, animalities and those who are other than human, sexual and bodily dissidence, from an anti-colonial stance. She is a member of the Colectivo Ayllu.

Natalia Rivera

They work with emerging digital and bio media, exploring the possibilities of digital technologies as a means of mutual support between living entities. In the context of indeterminate/queer knowledge creation, their processes are *undisciplinary*, open, collective, collaborative and community-based, through the Mutante lab and the Suratómica Network.

Pablo Selín

Programmer and artist from Santiago, Chile, living in Barcelona, Spain. Technical and/or creative collaborator in different artistic initiatives involving digital systems, visualisations and data management on the internet. He also participates in different video game and comic projects.
https://pabloselin.itch.io

Tatiana Avendaño

Bastard philosopher, raver and apprentice telepath. She forms part of the free, accessible festival Bogotrax, and was co-creator of the labSurlab World Media Labs Meeting. Through her Cuerpx Antenx project, she develops practices, protocols and thoughts that allow us to expand our bodies' capacity to emit and receive signals.
https://cuerpxantenx.xyz/

Tau Luna

(Medellín, 1989) is a visual artist, researcher, manager, curator and teacher. In their practice they research human migration as an event linked to colonial violence, and relationships between listening and memory with more-than-human migrant beings, through a cross of ancestral, scientific and intuitive technologies.

https://lunaacosta.net/

Thais de Menezes

Brazilian, researcher, independent curator, currently working between Europe and Brazil. Resident researcher at MACBA and member of the Independent Studies Programme at the same institution (Spain); founder and director of the platform ATRAVESSA, in the city of Porto (Portugal), and active in various other educational and social projects that deal with counter-coloniality.

val flores

Independent researcher, writer, teacher, sexual dissidence activist and performer. Her theoretical and poetic work is situated at the crossroads between feminist and queer pedagogical practices and artistic practices, interrogating writing and bodies in situations of (un) learning.

THIS BOOK WAS FINISHED
PRINT IN FEBRUARY 2024 WHEN THE
INTERNET CONSUMES MORE THAN
3% OF THE WORLD'S ELECTRICAL
ENERGY TO FUNCTION